IT Investment in Developing Countries: An Assessment and Practical Guideline

Sam Lubbe
Hi Agder College, Norway

IGP
IDEA GROUP PUBLISHING
Hershey USA • London UK

Senior Editor: Mehdi Khosrowpour
Managing Editor: Jan Travers
Copy Editor: Terry Heffelfinger
Typesetter: Marjaneh Talebi
Cover Design: Marjaneh Talebi
Printed at: BookCrafters

Published in the United States of America by
Idea Group Publishing
1331 E. Chocolate Avenue
Hershey PA 17033-1117
Tel: 717-533-8845
Fax: 717-533-8661
E-mail: jtravers@idea-group.com
Website: http://www.idea-group.com

and in the United Kingdom by
Idea Group Publishing
3 Henrietta Street
Covent Garden
London WC2E 8LU
Tel: 171-240 0856
Fax: 171-379 0609
http://www.eurospan.co.uk

Library of Congress Cataloging-in-Publication Data

Lubbe, Sam, 1952-
IT investment in developing countries: an assessment and practical guideline / Sam Lubbe.
p. cm.
ISBN 1-878289-55-1 (pbk.)
1. Information technology--Developing countries. 2. Information technology--Developing countries--Evaluation. I. Title.
HC59.72.I55L83 1998
303.48 ' 33 ' 091724--dc21
98-51687
CIP

British Cataloguing in Publication Data
A Cataloguing in Publication record for this book is available from the British Library.

IT Investment in Developing Countries: An Assessment and Practical Guideline

Table of Contents

Preface

Up to this stage, there has been no comprehensive guide for IT managers in developing countries. By guide, meaning how should these managers approach the investment in IT and how should they identify and manage the benefits and the IT investment of their organisation.

The book will thus address the assessment of the effectiveness of IT investment, the evaluation of IT investment and IT benefit management. However, this book uses an original approach to the assessment of the effectiveness of IT investment in developing countries and that no similar research, using this approach, exists. The aim of the book is, therefore, to address the approach and identify the assessment of the effectiveness of IT investment used by organisations, to develop a theory of good practice in this area; to test this thesis by reference to a focus group and practitioners; and thereby to develop the theory into a practical management guideline.

As will be seen in the first chapter, IT has been used to help manage resource creation for some time in developed countries and has been extensively used in developing countries over the past couple of years. This is a relatively new process sometimes referred to as part of the development programs of the developing countries.

The book began by using the case study method to collect evidence and content analysis was employed to analyse this evidence to identify empirical generalisations and thus, develop a theory of IT investment. IT investment evaluation and IT benefit identification. Correspondence analysis was used on the case study data as one step in establishing the theory. A focus group was used to verify the theory and the models that were created.

Finally the practical management guidelines suggested by the research and the models and content analysis figures were presented to practitioners as a cross validation process and the results reported. The results of this research is an objectively developed theory of how IT investments are formulated and evaluated and how IT investment benefits are identified, and a practical management guideline containing ten guidelines.

In all this book provides a step towards an evaluation of information technology investment, but cannot be regarded as a definitive work of this enormous subject. It contains some ideas that can be developed further by practical applications in industry. Many organisational executives will find both stimulating and useful. Perhaps this book might be considered a guide to measuring and managing IT investment and IT benefits.

Sam Lubbe (Ph.D.)
Information Systems
Hi Agder College (Kristiansand, Norway)

Acknowledgment

I would like to thank Dr Dan Remenyi for his encouragement throughout the research. I would also like to express my appreciation to him for the care and attention with which he has read the various drafts of this book and for the constructive criticism and suggestions he has made.

Furthermore I have received considerable encouragement and help from various colleagues at Vista University with the mathematical and statistical subjects whom were necessary for me to use in my analysis and for this I am most grateful. A special word of thank you to Mr Thierry Fahmy who supplied me with the software to conduct the correspondence analysis. Also a thank you to Mr Michael Venter for his patience in helping me to access extra space on the file-server and the instruction on the use of some of the software.

Throughout this research I have had various discussions with numerous business people, IS practitioners, consultants, librarians and other academics. All those involved have been most generous with the time they gave me for these discussions and use of resources. For this I would like to formally thank them.

I would like to thank Sue Nugus who so kindly proof read the book to find typing and spelling errors and who also helped with the typesetting.

Last but not least I would like to thank my family for all the support which they have given me during the research.

Finally, it is customary to acknowledge the ownership of the various trademarks and patents of the hardware and software products mentioned.

Chapter One

Introduction to the Issue of Information Technology Evaluation

Introduction

The evaluation of information systems (IS)[1] has gained considerable interest among academics, consultants and practitioners. The interest has resulted in an increasing belief that the current approach to IS management has to change (Remenyi & Money, 1994; Segars & Grover, 1994). IS are taking too long to develop, costing too much to produce and maintain and are frequently not perceived to be delivering the business benefits which were intended (Brynjolfsson & Hitt, 1993).

The interest in IS evaluation is primarily due to the large investment organisations have made in Information Technology (IT), and the strategic nature of the impact of IS on organisational performance (Segars & Grover, 1994). In addition, the fast moving business environment which many organisations face today cause IS professionals to complain that the goals set for them by management are changing. During the second half of the 1990s, it has become increasingly apparent that traditional IS methods are no longer appropriate to the way organisations conduct their business.

The book addresses the approach taken by organisations in a developing country to determine the effectiveness of their investment in IS. This chapter presents an overview of the current thinking about IT evaluation.

OVERVIEW

The overview of the issue underlining the subject of IS evaluation has been addressed in seven sections.

Background

Academics have been interested in IS evaluation since the beginning of the 1970s, and as time goes on, more and more work is being done in this area of interest. Hitt & Brynjolfsson (1996) argued that the result of the outcome of investments in IS depend on which question is being addressed and what data are being used. Ward *et al.* (1996) conducted a survey in the UK that examined how organisations went about the evaluation and realisation of information systems. They approached the survey by considering the overall process that benefits from a potential investment in IS are identified and appraised, realised in practice during a project, and evaluated post-project. They defined the overall process of evaluation and realisation[2] of IS benefits management as:

The process of organising and managing such that potential benefits arising from the use of IT are actually realised.

The need for evaluation

IT has changed the way in which organisations are doing business and the way in which they compete (Abdul-Gader & Kozar, 1995). IT is also seen as a fundamental method of gaining strategic and competitive advantage (Segars & Grover, 1994; Remenyi *et al.,* 1993). As a result, IT is playing an increasingly important role in organisations.

Organisations are continuing to invest large sums of money in IT in anticipation of a material return on investment (Willcocks & Lester, 1996). There is, however, doubt as to whether IT investment has proved economically successful at all. In South Africa, it has been estimated that close to R10 billion has been spent on IT during the last two years (Heafield, 1995). In many organisations, it represents the highest ongoing capital expenditure (Lubbe, 1994). IT investment is high and it is thus essential for managers in developing countries to be sure that investment in IT is economically justifiable. It is especially true for South Africa where reserves need to be carefully directed into the areas of high return so as to ensure economic growth, and therefore, support the country's Re-organisation and Development Programme (RDP).[3]

It is thus with the increasing amount of IT investment and substantial evidence of failures (Remenyi and Lubbe, 1998), together with claims of gaining competitive advantage, that there is some doubt as to what extent, if at all, the benefits of IT are being realised (Ward *et al.,* 1996). Many managers and researchers feel that IS evaluation has become a key management issue. These concerns provide an important rationale for the need of IT evaluation and thus a rationale for this book.

Evaluation of IT

Evaluation of IT investments has been the subject of much academic debate and literature in recent years. There are two main themes within the literature which are of relevance to the book, i.e., strategic information systems planning (SISP) and investment appraisal techniques for evaluating IT investments (Brynjolfsson & Hitt, 1993). Strategic information systems planning seeks to align IT investment with business strategies in order to maximise the opportunity for overall competitive advantage through IT. However, while the investment priorities for IT may then be determined, it is typically through individual IT investment projects that value to the organisation is realised in practice, i.e., investment appraisal techniques for evaluating IT are still required in addition to SISP. The life cycle emphasis placed on evaluation, by Ward *et al.* (1996), takes into account not only the pre-investment appraisal and post-implementation evaluation processes, but also how organisations do or do not ensure that the benefits claimed are actively managed through to realisation.

Evaluation of IT benefits is, in most cases within the current literature, concerned mainly with either the classification of types of benefits, or with the initial assessment and justification procedures for identifying and evaluating potential benefits which an IT project may deliver (Farbey *et al,* 1995a, 1995b). According to Remenyi & Sherwood-Smith (1996), the evaluation process requires active participation during project development from the primary stakeholders[4] including line managers and users, and a direct focus on business benefits realisation. It enables the finally commissioned IS to support the business or organisational objectives by realising the expected IS goals or outcomes. Traditional evaluation of IT investments can be likened to taking a single snapshot at a particular point in time; these snapshots are generally financially orientated or rely on some set of predetermined statistics. Remenyi & Sherwood-Smith (1996) argue that to ensure the success of an evaluation process it is necessary to establish that the primary stakeholders are represented by a team comprising representatives of the ultimate users, the management and the information systems developers. As part of their research, they developed an active benefit realisation (ABR) process. ABR is a process for ensuring that the IS which are ultimately delivered meet the organisation's current business requirements and in so doing, provide the best possible collection of specific processes and tools which may be used to maximise the potential business benefits within the information system's terms of reference.

Another approach to the apparent inadequacy of investment appraisal techniques has been to develop appraisal techniques such as information economics and return on management (Strassman, 1990). Ward *et al.* (1996) conclude that existing evaluation methods are considered to be unsatisfactory and are not applied widely or consistently. More sophisticated methods also do not appear to be the answer. They have decided to take an alternative approach, that of revisiting what constitutes a benefit, and how such a benefit could be realised.

IT implementation and benefits

IT implementation is usually brought about by a desire to improve business performance which it is believed will directly lead to the realisation of business benefits. Equally, Ward *et al.* (1996) note that it is recognised that IT on its own does not deliver benefits, what IT can do is to enable benefit opportunities. For an organisation to take advantage of these opportunities, changes must take place in the way that business activities are performed, as a result of the way that information is used. Benefits may therefore be considered as the effect of changes. Earl (1992) provides support for the view that benefits are associated with business change and not the technology itself. Organisations should agree what capabilities and actions, including IT, are needed to achieve the change, and then manage the change as a whole if full business benefits are to be delivered. If benefits are derived from IT through business changes, then it is reasonable to assume that the implications of these changes be assessed before the project is started in order to quantify the potential benefits (Barua *et al.* 1995).

The process model and benefits management

A process model (Figure 1.1) was developed as part of a research programme conducted at Cranfield Business School in the United Kingdom (Ward *et al.*, 1996) The model was derived from an analysis of the context within which benefits management is required. It was developed from other models of planned business improvement such as total quality management and existing work on benefits management within the NHS[5]. The model has been tested and refined in reviews of actual IT projects within the health organisations and forms the basis of best practice guidelines on benefits management.

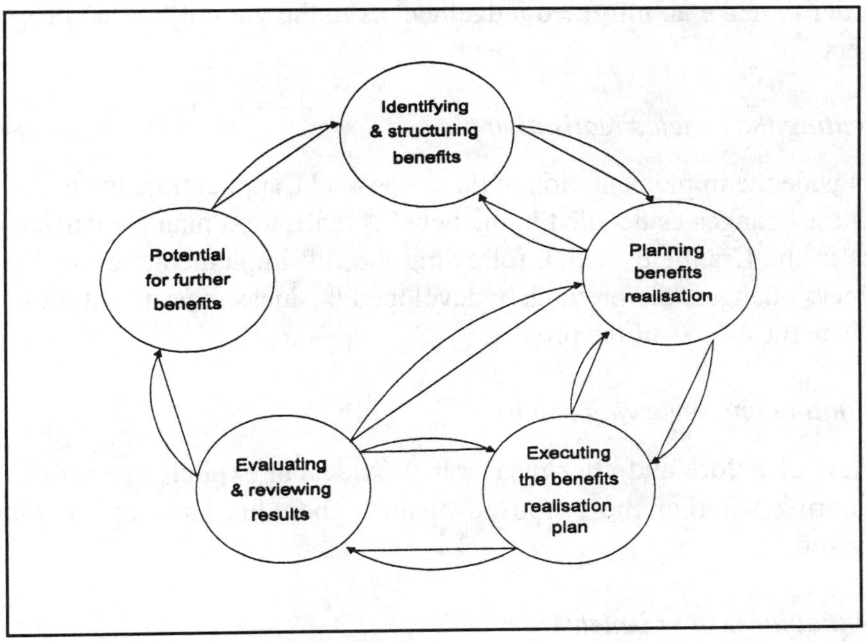

Figure 1.1: A process model of benefits management (Ward et al: 1996)

The elements of the Cranfield business process model shown in Figure 1.1 are described below.

Identifying and structuring benefits

The proposed benefits are identified and, for each proposed benefit, suitable business measures are developed. According to the model, the benefits are structured in order to understand the linkages between technology effects, business changes and overall business effects. Specific responsibility for realising the benefits is allocated within the business according to the model.

Planning benefits realisation

The full costs of both IT development and business changes can be assessed, in order to make an informed judgement as to the viability of the proposed project.

Executing the benefits realisation plan.

Alongside the implementation of the proposed IT application, the necessary business changes as detailed in the benefits realisation plan are carried out. Thus in the Cranfield model, following the full implementation of IT and business changes, the previously developed business measures are used to evaluate the effects of the project.

Evaluating and reviewing results.

Review of before and after measures provides an explicit mechanism for evaluating whether the proposed business benefits have actually been delivered.

Potential for further benefits

As a result of the post-project review, it may become apparent that further benefits are now achievable, which were not envisaged at the outset. This stage provides the opportunity to plan for, and realise, these further benefits.

Benefits management

Ward *et al.* (1996) were motivated by a belief that the scope of current approaches, methodologies and processes usually fail to address the management of business change adequately, with a consequent significant loss of potential benefit to the organisation. Hitt & Brynjolfsson (1996) demonstrated that the relevance of an IT investment should be related to productivity, improved business profitability and value for customers. They argued that IT could have increased productivity but there is no empirical connection between the provided substantial benefits and higher business profits. Newton (1995) notes that all methods for planning and managing IT activities, underline the need to base IT investment decisions on the expected input on business objectives and performance. The importance of benefits is increasing, he argues, as the management of IT matures and as senior management becomes more aware of the IT issues.

Newton (1995) argued that the treatment of non-economic[6] benefits is becoming more sophisticated and objective. The assessment of financial benefits, he claims, is becoming more focused and is accountable under the economic processes of all organisations. Newton (1995) states that to manage benefits objectively and consistently, organisations need a benefits framework that sets out how any IT investment will be assessed. Hitt & Brynjolfsson (1996) found that IT investment had a significant impact on organisational output. Lubbe (1994) and Abdul-Gader & Kozar (1995) also reported this in their studies. However, Hitt & Brynjolfsson (1996) estimated that the benefit to consumers could be substantial.

The survey by Ward *et al.* (1996) shows that around 50% of organisations have methodologies for either IT systems development, project management or investment appraisal; though only 20% of those have all three. A minority of organisations consider these methodologies to be effective in ensuring successful IS. Few organisations have a methodological approach to benefits management, and the majority of respondents agreed that there is room for improvement in their current benefits management practices.

Though most of the respondents in the Ward *et al.* (1996) survey express confidence that IT is delivering benefits to their organisation, further analysis of their responses reveals little grounds for their confidence. Success criteria in terms of benefits delivered are the exception rather than the rules, and in many cases measures of project success are defined after project implementation or not at all. Ward *et al.* (1996) claim that few organisations allocate specific responsibility to managers for realising the benefits claimed in a project justification, and few produce a benefits delivery plan. Many of the respondents openly admitted that their current project justification processes overstate the benefits in order to get approval; hence, benefits are claimed which are unlikely to be achieved in practice. A wide range of industry sectors participated in the survey, including construction, financial services, food and drink, etc.

The top issues, which the survey respondents currently face, are benefits management, and alignment of IT with business strategy and objectives. Strategy was the single most important issue in the majority of cases, thus supporting a need for SISP (Remenyi & Sherwood-Smith, 1996). However, SISP will not guarantee the delivery of benefits. The current benefits that are perceived to be provided by IT were heavily biased towards cost savings. Improved management information systems was perceived to be a major benefit, with improved business efficiency, and the ability to support business change and growth. The underlying issues which drive any organisational investment in IT showed that cost reduction and profit improvement was still an important driver, followed by improved process efficiency (Lubbe, 1994).

Hitt & Brynjolfsson (1996) argue that it is important how IT investment affects the organisation. It is possible for organisations to realise productivity benefits from effective management of IT without having to translate these benefits into profits. Also, some organisations are making IT investments necessary to maintain competitive parity, but are not able to gain competitive advantage.

Techniques and responsibilities for IT benefit realisation

Cost-benefit analysis (CBA) and return on investment (ROI) were the most commonly mentioned appraisal techniques for deciding upon IT investments (Lubbe *et al.,* 1995; Ward *et al.,* 1996)[7]. More than half the respondents mentioned formal techniques such as pay back, ROI, internal rate of return, or net present value. Common problems with the methods were that they were unable to take account of the full range of potential benefits, especially intangible benefits and some respondents claimed that the wrong projects were approved as a result. Projects often have benefits that are not tangible in nature (e.g., improved staff morale). Most of the respondents believe that their current project justification process fails to identify all available benefits (Lubbe, 1994) implying that not only are benefits claimed that are unlikely to be realised in practice, but also that the process itself places greater emphasis on getting approval than on delivering any proposed benefits. An indication was that the purpose of carrying out pilot studies is not always clear, and in the majority of cases, the primary purpose does not appear to be to obtain a better understanding of potential benefits or how to realise them (Hitt & Brynjolfsson, 1996).

Newton (1995) argues that organisations should decide how they will treat IT investment benefits and how they want to balance the different perspectives of benefits. Newton (1995) notes that IT cannot be isolated from business processes, and hence policies on IT benefits will impact changes in the roles and responsibilities for business operations.

The majority of respondents interviewed by Ward *et al.* (1996) believe that it is not possible to anticipate all benefits at the project approval stage. The implication is that there are often more benefits to be gained after implementation, but that current practices mitigate against exploring these potential further benefits. There appears to be a potential paradox between the current confidence that IT is delivering benefits to the organisation and the view that there is significant scope for improvement in how benefits are being realised. This may be explained by the nature of the benefits that respondents perceived were actually delivered, and a view that much greater potential exists to deliver other types of benefit; or that only a proportion of the benefits that were actually delivered and that more could be delivered with a more effective process (Ward *et al.,* 1996).

Ward *et al.* (1996) came to the following conclusions.

- Few organisations have a complete or comprehensive management process to ensure the proposed benefits from IT investments are actually realised.

- Just over half of the organisations have formal methodologies for systems development, project management and investment appraisal; however, only 20% have implemented all three of these.

- The results confirm the findings of previous researchers that existing methods, including investment appraisal, are deemed generally unsatisfactory in identifying all available benefits or adequately quantifying the benefits.

- Although improved investment appraisal techniques are likely to improve the decision-making process for IT investments, on their own they are unlikely to ensure that the benefits claimed for those investments are realised.

Hitt & Brynjolfsson (1996) suggested that:

- When cost is the central strategic issue in an industry, the productivity result suggest that IT investment may be one way to pursue a cost leadership strategy.

- Managers seeking higher profits should look beyond productivity to focus on how IT can address other strategic levers such as customer service.

- IT spending alone is not determinative of success.

SUMMARY AND CONCLUSION

The effectiveness of IT investment has gained considerable interest among researchers, consultants and practitioners. This interest is due to the large investments that organisations have made in IT; the increasingly strategic nature of the impact of IT on organisational performance; the realisation or otherwise of both efficiency and effectiveness benefits and no apparent consensus for the definition of IT success. Despite this interest there seems to be little agreement on how to evaluate the effectiveness of an IT investment. The next chapter reviews how the role and function of IT and IS[8] have developed over the last eight years and how IT investment appraisal have been raised by academics in the field. It discusses some recent research in the field and defines some of the issues to be addressed in the book.

ENDNOTES

[1] The evaluation of an IS means determining that system's value/worth. The process involves understanding, assessing and measuring the system. Evaluation may either be a conscious or unconscious process (Remenyi & Sherwood-Smith, 1996). In the context of this chapter the evaluation process is a conscious, formal procedure.

[2] Benefit realisation was perhaps first addressed by Earl (1992) and by Farbey et al. (1992). Remenyi & Sherwood-Smith (1996) also pick this issue up. Ward et al. (1996) emphasised the importance of it in their paper. Benefit realisation implies that a new focus, which encompasses concentrating on and understanding the business, issues and how the information system delivers real value to the organisation.

[3] The RDP is an upliftment programme created by the government of national unity to enable the disenfranchised population of SA access to services such as housing, electricity and running water and similar programmes are being followed by other developing countries.

[4] Primary stakeholders include people who will be directly involved with the IS as managers, users, technicians, etc.

[5] NHS is the abbreviation for the National Health Service in the United Kingdom of Great Britain and Northern Ireland. The central team created an internal document on benefits management for hospital information support systems.

[6] Non-economic benefits are those benefits that managers should address when assessing the financial benefits of IT investments. Newton's (1995) notion of non-economic benefits are those benefits that cannot be measured in traditional financial terms. These were described by Newton as quantity of work processed, volume of publications, technical correctness, presentation, etc.

[7] CBA includes concepts such as return on investments (ROI) and other concepts such as discounted cost flows (DCF), net present value (NPV), etc.

[8] Some researchers make a clear distinction between IT and IS. Such authors claim that the term IT represents hardware and that the term IS represents software. However, the author of this book regards the term IT as representing all computer equipment, software and people expenses.

REFERENCES

Abdul-Gader A.H. & Kozar K.A. (1995). "The impact of Computer Alienation of Information Technology Investment Decisions: An exploratory cross-national analysis", *MIS Quarterly*, December, 535–559.

Barua A., Kriebel C.H. & Mukhopadhyay T. (1991). "An Economic Analysis of Strategic Information Technology investments", *MIS Quarterly*, September, 313–331.

Brynolfson E. & Hitt L.M. (1993). "Is Information Systems spending productive? New evidence and new results", *Proceedings of the International Conference on Information Systems*, Orlando Florida USA, 47–64.

Earl M.J. (1992). "Putting IT in its place: a polemic for the nineties", *Journal of Information Technology*, No 7, 100–108.

Farbey B., Land F. & Targett D. (1992). "Evaluating investments in IT", *Journal of Information Technology*, No. 7, 109–122.

Farbey B., Land F. & Targett D. (1995a). "A taxonomy of information systems applications: the benefits' evaluation ladder," *European Journal of Information Systems*, No 4, 41–50.

Farbey B., Land F. & Targett D. (1995b). "System - Method - Context: a contribution towards the development of guidelines for choosing a method of evaluating I/S investment", *Proceedings of the 2nd Henley Conference on the Evaluation of IT Investments*, Henley Management College, Henley, UK, 267–276.

Heafield A. (1995). *The evaluation of IS Success*, Masters research dissertation, Department of Information Systems, University of the Witwatersrand, Johannesburg.

Hitt L.M & Brynjolfson E. (1996). "Productivity, Business Profitability, and Consumer Surplus: Three Different Measures of Information Technology Value," *MIS Quarterly*, June 121 – 141.

Lubbe S.I. (1994). *The impact of Information Technology (IT) on the financial performance of organisations in a developing country*, M.Com.-Thesis, UCT, Cape Town.

Lubbe S.I., Eggett R. & Hawkes N. (1995). Determining the significance of Decision Criteria in the Selection of IT investments in South Africa, *Information Technology for Developing Countries,* December.

Newton K. (1995). "Corporate Versus Business Area benefits from IT - Practical experience from the Public sector", *Proceedings of the 2nd European Conference on Information Technology Investment,* Henley Management College, Henley UK,1 - 11.

Remenyi Dan, and Lubbe Sam (1998). "Some information system issues in South Africa and suggestions as to how to deal with them." Unpublished report (awaiting details of acceptance).

Remenyi D., Money A. & Twite A. (1993). *A guide to Measuring and Managing IT Benefits,* Second Edition, NCC Blackwell Oxford

Remenyi D. & Money, A. (1994). "Service quality and corre.spondence analysis in determining problems with the effective use of Computer Services," *European Journal of Information systems*, 3(1), 2 – 12.

Remenyi D. & Sherwood-Smith M. (1996). *Active benefits realization using a formative evaluation approach*, International Turnkey Systems, Kuwait.

Segars A.H. & Grover, V. (1994). "Strategic Group Analysis: A methodological approach for exploring the industry level impact of information technology", *Omega*, 22(1) in OR/MS Alert # 3, September 1994, 1 - 6.

Strassman P.A.(1990). *The Business Value of Computers: An executive's guide*, Information Economics Press, Connecticut.

Ward J. Taylor P. & Bond P. (1996). "Evaluation and realisation of IS/IT Benefits: an empirical study of current practices", *European Journal of Information Systems,* 4, 214 – 225.

Willcocks L. & Lester S. (1996). "*The evaluation and management of information systems investments: from feasibility to routine operations",* Chapter in a book edited by Willcocks L. Investing in Information Systems: Evaluation and Management, Chapman & Hall.

Chapter Two

Past Attempts to Measure IT Investment Effectiveness

Introduction

Remenyi & Williams (1995) state that an extensive literature review is a prerequisite for sound academic research. This book does not claim to review all the available studies that have attempted to measure the effectiveness of IT investment, but rather focuses on a number of the more recent papers and some books that have made a contribution to the field of the assessment of IT investment effectiveness.

This chapter therefore reviews the literature since 1990 and considers thinking on the subject of IT investment. In so doing, it provides a background to the problem of assessing the economic and the financial dimensions of IT[1]. The need to define the value of information is also addressed in this chapter because it is necessary for purposes of IT costs classification and the effective employment of IT. Attempts to assess the value of the intangible benefits of IT (including the effect of expenditure, such as research and development) are discussed.

The appropriateness of using models which can establish IT investment measures (e.g., Cotten & Hogbin, 1995), are reviewed. The chapter also considers some authors' claims that there is no correlation between IS effectiveness and corporate performance (Carlson & McNurlin, 1992). Finally, some of the shortcomings of these studies are reviewed. The literature review has been produced by theme and within theme order they are in date order. Since the length of this book is limited, some research had to be omitted. The author has identified only 13 themes from the research which are:

1. definition of the value of information;

2. the business value of IT;

3. managing IT benefits;
4. justifying IT investments;
5. IT and business change;
6. a comparison between IT and other investments;
7. IT and capital justification;
8. hidden costs and IT investments;
9. cost-benefit analysis of IT investment;
10. the profit impact of IT investment;
11. economic characteristics of IT investment;
12. quantifying the business value of IT; and
13. evaluation of IT.

Need for defining *value of information*

Since the book focuses on assessing the effectiveness of IT investment, the term *value of information* requires clarification and consideration.

Definition of the value of information

The approach of Ahituv & Neumann (1990) to the value of information is related to the user of information, when the information is used, and in what situation the information is used. They argue that information does not have an absolute universal value and any attempt to assess the value of information should be closely tied to the decisions, which are supported by the use of the information. Glazer (1993) defines the value of information as the sum of profits from increased revenues and reduced costs of future transactions as a result of information collected during the transaction. He also includes in his notion of the value of information profits from the sale of the information itself. Information is a valuable resource and is characterised as an ordinary financial resource. These views were found to be fairly wide ranging and they can be summarised and combined to provide the following definition:

The value of information is the sum of profits from increased revenues and reduced costs of present and future transactions as a result of information collected and used during transactions while effectively employing IT; and the profits from the sale of the information.

Previous research on IT investment

The business value of IT

Ahituv & Neumann (1990) noted that any attempt to assess the value of information should be linked to a decision supported by the information provided. They emphasise the need to employ economic criteria in IS planning and development and recorded difficulties involved in assessing the costs and benefits of information. According to them, economic criteria should include a comprehensive range of costs, one of which is the cost of IT research and development, because these can affect benefits which the organisation receives in the long run.

Ahituv & Neumann (1990) further suggest that the selection of criteria to be used in comparative analysis and the performance of numerically based economic or financial calculations is the easier part of cost-benefit analysis (CBA). The difficult part of the evaluation exercise, they argue, is to identify all the elements that constitute costs and benefits and to determine how to measure (or estimate) all these elements. They thus classify costs as falling under the following categories: tangible monetary costs, tangible non-monetary costs[2]; and intangible costs. Like most other authors, Ahituv & Neumann focus on tangible benefits and pay little attention to intangible benefits. Furthermore, the last category was sub-divided into costs that can be translated into monetary terms and those that cannot.

The Butler-Cox Foundation (1990) stated that obtaining value from IT is probably one of the main concerns of business managers. According to them, there is, unfortunately, no single measure that can be used to conclusively prove the business value of IT expenditure. They note, however, that by relating the expenditure to a range of business-performance measures, the value of IT investments could be assessed at least as well as that of other investments. Obtaining value from IT is critically dependent on how IT investment decisions are made, and means recognising that different evaluation criteria are applicable to different IT investments. For most types of IT investment, cost-benefit analysis is insufficient and management judgement should be applied as well. Furthermore, the Butler-Cox Foundation (1990) points out that IT investment proposals could also take account of the prevailing corporate climate, which means that systems directors should be sensitive to the realities of corporate politics.

Butler-Cox Foundation (1990), which has a prescriptive tone, noted that management's judgement is an essential element of the evaluation process. They argue that IT resources should be linked to business priorities. Organisations should allocate limited resources to provide the best return on expenditure. The IT committee would recognise benefits and ensures that they reach or obtain these benefits. The organisation has to ensure that they appoint people with the right skills and train managers to ensure that the above are reached.

Glazer (1993) notes that firms which successfully integrate an IT strategy with their business strategies do so by focusing on the information itself as the real carrier of value and source of competitive advantage, rather than on technology. He states that organisations, which successfully use IT for competitive advantage, are unusual. It is because they approach the application of IT from a different perspective, and because they recognise information as the organisation's primary asset, that IT becomes the mechanism through which the organisation is able to link IT strategy to business strategy. Glazer (1993) states that a primary mechanism whereby a firm becomes an information-intensive organisation is the implementation of a procedure for measuring the value of its information assets.

Glazer (1993) measures the value of information by using a technique that bases the value of information on the transaction. The components of value may be: to generate additional revenues by attracting new customers; to generate additional revenues by extracting higher prices from customers; to reduce finance costs; etc. The conclusion he came to is that:

organisations that are acclaimed as leading the way in information-based strategies appear to be doing so more through an implicit understanding of the information-valuation processes outlined, rather than through its concrete full-fledged realisation.

In a paper on measuring technology's business value, Katz (1993) believes that organisations seek to prove IT benefits. Some methods used by managers to measure the business value of IT are: measuring the impact on customers, return-on-investment (ROI) calculations, and gut reaction. It can be assumed that a single measurement of the business value of IT may be arbitrary and cannot include all the factors that contribute to its impact on the business. Little direct evidence is available on the relationship between IT investment and performance. Also, relationships found cannot be generalised beyond the particular industry because of different methods of measuring IT investment and organisational performance. Katz (1993) argues that the need to measure the business value of IT could be driven by two possibilities: that IT expenditures could have reached a threshold level in the organisation that triggers the concern of senior managers; and that managers are interested in determining the contribution and costs of IS as part of the process of considering outsourcing as a way to reduce IT expenditure in line with restructuring the organisation.

Katz (1993) claims that IT assessment could be a function of the stage of development of IS in the organisation, the size of the organisation, the level of senior managers' understanding of IT and the level of technology comfort of business managers. He notes that a reasonable prototype model for measuring the business value of IT can be derived from the work of previous researchers. Katz (1993) found that IT expenditure has reached a threshold level in organisations that triggers the concern of managers in addressing investment decisions among different stakeholders. Managers would also like to reduce IT expenditure in line with restructuring the organisation. He concludes that IT investments continue to be of importance for organisations and that an answer needs to be found for all these issues.

In a study on the business value of IT, Mukhopadhyay *et al.* (1995) stated that a great deal of controversy exists around the impact of IT on organisational performance. They note that while some authors have reported positive impacts, others have found negative or no impacts. Further, IT has become a matter of concern for managers today. However, they note that the spectacular growth of IT has potential for improving the performance of organisations. Mukhopadhyay *et al.* (1995) claim that investment in IT puts increasing pressure on managers to justify the outlay by quantifying the business value of IT. They argue that major investments in IT demand an analysis of costs and benefits, plus strategic considerations. Integration of IT applications with internal systems should be considered.

Managing IT benefits

The generic benefits of IT and IS are efficiency, effectiveness and strategic advantage. In theory, these generic benefits could be assessed in terms of the usual financial measures of business performance. In practice, however, it is difficult to measure benefits due to the growing importance of the *soft* benefits of IT/IS, and to a changing business environment. The level of IT investment is rising and organisations will need better tools to assess and monitor the benefits of IT/IS.

Some ways of justifying expenditure on IT/IS projects are: investments are unavoidable and can not be justified formally; the investment is justified as an act of faith based on the judgement of senior managers; the causal logic by which a business improvement will arise from the proposed IS is identified as the basis for the business case; the size of the change is estimated and is checked quantitatively when the system is in operation; the quantified change is given some considered weighting, so that disparate benefits can be compared with each other; and each of the benefits is given a financial value so that they can be compared with each other. An organisation should recognise the generic benefits of IT/IS and the different types of business case appropriate for each IT/IS. Benefits should also be managed and identified before the time.

There is widespread and continuing interest in IS and its effects on business strategy, particularly when it can confer a sustainable advantage for innovative organisations. An important characteristic of IT is its ability to manage interactions among economic activities. Therefore, it can be argued that economic theory can be used to establish a link between characteristics of IT and shifts in resource values.

IT equipment and services are available to all organisations. Most of this IT could be duplicated by other organisations that can then be in a position to offer comparable services at lower costs. Specifically:

IT can lead to sustainable competitive advantage when it is used to leverage differences in strategic resources.

The economic interaction allows managers to identify and examine some opportunities for deploying IT to leverage structural resource differences among organisations. IT resources may be expensive for small organisations, but they are seldom expensive for major players. Benefits resulting from an innovative application of IT can be better defended if the system exploits unique resources of the organisation. IT can also change the value of resources by reducing the cost of integrating and coordinating economic activities and can increase the potential production economies such as scale, scope and specification.

Ward *et al.* (1995) state that many organisations have methodologies for systems development, project management and investment appraisal. These methodologies were, however, deemed far from satisfactory in ensuring that benefits are properly identified and realised, thereby echoing the view of most of the authors reviewed.

Ward *et al.* (1995) found that few organisations had a complete or comprehensive management process to ensure that the proposed benefits from IT/IS are actually realised, while just over half the organisations that participated in their survey had some form of investment appraisal. They claim that improved investment appraisal techniques are likely to improve the IS/IT investment decision-making process. In isolation, however, appraisal techniques are unlikely to ensure that benefits claimed for investments are realised.

Justifying IT investments

Dealing with technological advances has been and continues to be a key facet of the IS manager's job as new IT continues to be introduced at a rapid rate. It can be noted that the economic question regarding IT investment is a problem faced by all managers and some investments in IT are based on gut feelings rather than hard evidence. All IT investments, however, should be treated as future investments which can greatly increase the estimated pre-investment value of a new IT project.

Managers have a problem investing in IT justifying these investments. It is especially a problem for IT investments as it is even more difficult to determine their value using traditional capital-budgeting approaches. One problem in using a net present value approach to evaluate new IT investments is in the determination of an appropriate discount rate for these new projects. Also, investment in a technology project can be compared to buying a call option on a traded security in that it provides the organisation with an option to invest in future projects that can generate revenues by acquiring the underlying securities in which the option is written. The value of future IT investments may be determined by using models similar to those that are used to price options in securities. The use of options pricing models to determine the value of other types of IT investments should be investigated.

Deitz & Renkema (1995) claim that IT investment decisions remain difficult in terms of assessing the associated costs, benefits and risks and effectively managing the underlying decision-making process. The number of methods which aim to support these decisions are large and increasing. They argue that the apparent gap between the many methods for IT investment planning and justification and decision-making processes can be traced back to prevailing methods that almost exclusively take formal-rational arguments into account. These methods do not recognise the complexity and diversity of IT investment decisions in a wider organisational context, nor the several levels of investment decision making and their interdependencies that can be distinguished in practice.

It was also noted by Deitz & Renkema (1995) that findings from previous studies lead them to conclusions such as: the financial perspective with IT investments seems to be of statistical importance, but only of limited impact in practice, while strategic arguments are perceived as critical; the IT specific methods for supporting decisions on IT investments are rarely used and it is even argued that the justified procedures are merely rituals, do not meet analytical standards and are often of an ad-hoc character. Despite these deficiencies there is no clear evidence that practitioners are particularly dissatisfied with their current approach. Deitz & Renkema (1995) argue that although a financial cost benefit analysis is often carried out, it becomes clear that non-quantitative and non-rational aspects (e.g. politics) are of major importance in IT investment decisions.

Deitz & Renkema (1995) identified different levels for IT investment decision making. Some of these are: individual investment projects like ROI, internal rate of return (IRR) and ++ (NPV); the portfolio-level where ranking or portfolio methods play a role; and the budget-level (prioritising a budget for specific functions). Deitz & Renkema (1995) suggest that additional case study research is needed to increase understanding of the factors that shape decision-making practices used to justify IT investments. It can help gain insight between the quality of IT investment decisions and the way decisions are made.

IT and business change

Earl (1992) argues that IT is undergoing heavy scrutiny and sometimes-radical surgery. IT budgets are continually being capped or pruned, IT operations and development are being outsourced and IT directors are being replaced. Chief executives are growing tired of IT rhetoric and hype; many of them feel it has been oversold and under delivered. He states that although it was argued in the 80's that IT investment could bring about business benefits, investment in IT alone usually yields little return.

Other changes were also required if substantial business benefit was to be earned. A viewpoint, portrayed by Earl (1992), is that the organisation should identify business change needs first. They should agree what capabilities and actions, including IT, are needed to achieve the change and then manage it as a whole if full business benefits are to be delivered. Another perspective on value could be the cost of not investing in IT. Earl (1992) suggests that a portion of the IT budget should be allowed for prototyping and experimentation by users and joint IS-user teams when interesting ideas arise.

Earl (1992) noted that the 80's were characterised by rapid developments in IT, rising IT expenditures in organisations and high hopes about the payoff of IT investments. This optimistic view has changed in the 1990's as IT expenditure is no longer rising. Value for money questions are asked about IT and changes are being made to IT in organisational structures. Earl (1992) states that if an IT investment is an integral part of a vision of the future of an organisation, justification is simplified because organisations should understand why the IT investment is proposed and they may already be committed to it. He emphasised that it is important to integrate IT with the organisation. IT could be a tool for change in organisations in the future and these concepts needs to be kept in mind when an IT investment is to be considered.

A comparison between IT and other investments

Powell (1992) compared IT investment with normal investments to see whether they differed. He notes that IT investments are undertaken because organisations want to gain competitive advantage, to improve productivity, to enable new ways of managing and organising, and to develop new business. However, each IT investment has some economic underpinning. The problem of IT appraisal is that it is difficult to quantify benefits and problems. On the other hand, Powell (1992) states that there are probably few investments that are as difficult to evaluate.

Applying objective methods to evaluate IT investments, management will endeavour to categorise the costs associated with a system or proposed system. The same objective methods could be used to categorise benefits (e.g., cost-benefit analysis, systems analysis, and Delphi evidence). Objective systems will try to assess and predate the system, while, on the other hand, subjective IT investment evaluation methods are merely spurious, pseudo-quantitative ones. Using the subjective method to IT investment evaluation the organisation should try to quantify benefits in order to differentiate between systems, but the quantification is in fact of feelings, attitudes and perceptions. Subjective systems are used only *ex post* in investment evaluations.

Powell (1992) claims that there seems to be almost a blind acceptance that IT investment is different, but it does not seem to be a tested hypothesis. He argues that the problems with IT investment are the same as normal investments and therefore, the solutions may also be the same. Solutions suggested include accepting that IT investment is not different and that standard techniques are as applicable to IT as to any other type of project. The alternative could be to accept that IT is different and hence not quantifiable. Lastly, Powell (1992) suggests that a new methodology be developed but the field is overcrowded with nearly 20 models and that a new model is likely to add little to present knowledge. However, he suggests that a last attempt be made to see how current techniques could be used to overcome present problems.

IT and capital justification

Clemons & Weber (1990) argued that strategic IT programmes often lack formal economic justification. They note that difficulties in justifying an investment that has since proved its value are not surprising. User adoption, future benefits, and competitive impact are difficult to forecast. They claim that as the strategic importance of IT increases the decision of where and when to allocate resources to IT programmes has become risky and difficult.

Clemons & Weber (1990) note that although executives are tempted by the opportunities for strategic impact, they struggle with the amount of expenditure and uncertainty associated with the investment. They also note that IT can confer an advantage under appropriate conditions and even when it fails, it may still prove crucial (threshold investments). They suggest that both these concepts—competitive advantage and strategic necessity - confound traditional financial analysis. In practice, many organisations misapply discounted cash flow models to IT investments. They also point out that benefits that are not easily measured tend to be ignored and set to nil. Financial analysis also tended to focus too narrowly on labour and material savings. To compensate for high-perceived risk, rates-of-return hurdles were set at arbitrarily high levels.

Clemons & Weber (1990) stated that direct-cost savings and higher production rates that once covered the cost of an IT investment in a short time are no longer sufficient to cover the high costs of new information technology. Justification for IT investments include quality and better customer service and there are no general acceptable decisions available. Managers also struggle to evaluate new technology investments and thinks that technology has fallen short of their expectations.

In a paper on capital budgeting in IS development, Tam (1992) states that senior MIS personnel and managers have indicated that capital budgeting has little impact on IS investment. Also, simple techniques such as payback period and cost-benefit ratios are preferred over sophisticated discounted cash-flow models. Problems with cost and return estimations are shown to be the key factors that limit this model's use. He suggests that the decision authority vary according to the project value and the type of decisions being taken.

Some findings by Tam (1992) are: capital budgeting techniques are used but have a minor impact on the evaluation, termination, and post-audit of IS-projects; simple budgeting techniques are preferred over complex discounted cash-flow techniques; strategic value is reported as an important criterion in evaluating IS projects; and the more familiar IS staff are with capital budgeting techniques, the less they rely on top managers to evaluate IS projects. His research delivered empirical evidence that capital budgeting techniques are not in use in IS investment. Sutherland (1993) who conducted a similar study in the South African Province of Gauteng supported this finding.

Tam (1992) suggested that the major problem with capital budgeting techniques is an estimation of cost and return on investment. He proposed that an organisation's cost of capital should be used as a discount rate for IT capital budgeting techniques. Issues such as project priority change and technical problems are the cause of project termination decisions.

Hidden costs and IT investments

In a paper on the hidden investment in IT, Kaye *et al.* (1995) note that the expansion of computing has altered the way organisations work. However, they argue that while processing costs have fallen, it has been accompanied by increasing spending on technology. Another problem lies in comparing alternative systems, as it is not possible to find a common accounting technique that takes all factors into account. They note that if an organisation considers an investment in IT as a unique occurrence, it should ensure that it includes costs and benefits, whether hidden or not. They argue that all IT investments include hidden costs, whether they are a replacement of, or an addition to, existing technology.

Kaye *et al.* (1995) note that the evaluation of IT investments relies on the satisfactory assessment of costs and benefits, but the full impact of these are not fully understood. The visible aspects of costs and benefits often cloak a hidden dimension. The tangible costs and benefits address the parts of an IT investment decision which the manager can easily identify and attach a quantifiable value to it. On the other hand, the intangible elements emphasise the costs and benefits of an investment which commonly do not have a physical form and are accounted for in terms of some expected future value, rather than past cost. Current approaches, to investment appraisal, and the general accounting culture, emphasise a sort-term perspective that focuses on a single investment. Post event evaluation take two forms, either as a blame allocation exercise, which creates a climate suppressing IT development, or a culture of learning which honours learning from mistakes.

Some authors (Katz, 1993; Ward *et al.*, 1995) have observed that it is difficult to assign a value to some of the benefits that an organisation could receive from an investment in IT. It is also difficult to price computer services because of the existence of intangible benefits. However, it is possible to reduce the risk involved in doing value analysis of benefits by treating each IT investment as a portfolio investment with its own risk attached to it. Hidden costs (e.g., back-up time) were noted to be an important aspect ignored by some IT departments (Kaye *et al.*, 1995). It is also not possible to compare systems because of different accounting methods and problems experienced.

Authors such as Clemons (1991) and Earl (1992) noted that most surveys underestimate total investment in IT. Mukhopadhyay *et al.* (1995) agree that a formal model should be created to evaluate IT investments. Authors such as Clemons (1991) and Deitz & Renkema (1995) suggested that an IT investment has an associated level of risk. There are also lots of models available to assess IT investments, but it is not clear which ones are the best to use (Deitz & Renkema, 1995).

Attempts to measure IT investment and the benefits it imparts to the organisation

Various approaches were used by researchers such as Esther & Brooke (1995) to measure the benefits that an organisation receives. Some of these approaches are discussed below.

Cost-benefit analysis for IT investment

Peters (1990) developed an evaluation methodology for specific IT investments. His methodology deals with the development of a cost-benefit hierarchy for project evaluation. The cost-benefit hierarchy has the following attributes:

- Variables are identified at the lowest key. These variables are measurable indicators that may have physical or cost performance characteristics. The nature of these key variables is that they are measurable (e.g., stock turnover, customer queuing time). Peters (1990) notes that the existence of measurable variables dispels the concern that unquantifiable benefits are stated in support of investments.

- Cost-benefit components can be divided into two separate streams, similar to a balance sheet.

Peters (1990) claims that planned initiatives are subjected to a stage, whereby the investments are mapped. Each investment is scored for its benefits and orientation areas. These could be plotted on a grid to give a map of planned projects. Using this map and after discussion with senior managers, a summarised map could be drawn and the IT strategy plotted on the same grid. The proposed strategy could be compared and decisions taken to go ahead with the planned investment.

The next step is to identify the key variables of investments by user departments who would act as lead sponsors for the investments. These variables would be tabled, discussed and impact areas identified. A possible cost saving or generation of income could be calculated and the overall impact assessed in the form of a decision tree drawing. Managers should be closely involved with these decisions.

Some of the advantages of using the methodology of Peters (1990) are that:

- it covers the complete range of evaluation stages from the initial identification of investments to the management of benefits identified;
- it identifies an early evaluation process;
- it contains the parameters of benefits and orientation; and
- it gives little importance to the internal rate of return as a means of investment appraisal.

The profit impact of IT

Harris & Katz (1991) note that there is an increased incentive to examine the link between business strategy and the information strategy. They assessed the sophistication of systems technology by using a table of the types of data processing installations. Table 2.1, formulated by a panel of senior IS executives, has rows which correspond to five levels of system technology sophistication. The rows characterise the sophistication of systems technology according to: (i) hardware environment, (ii) operations, (iii) systems software, (iv) application software, and (v) management. Each organisation selects their data processing installation based on the definitions that are supplied with the survey instrument.

Additionally, Harris & Katz (1991) plot the income versus operating expense over a couple of years. The sample is ranked by income and divided into quintiles and the result of the exercise is portrayed in a tabular form, comparing the premium income, average non-interest operating expense and average amount spent on IT. Another plotted graph shows income growth versus non-interest operating expense for the sample used by them.

Hardware	Multiple processors/Multiple locations Directly connected or via switched networks
Operational	Database management system, TSO, CICS, remote and local batch
Systems Software	Multiple CPUs/Multiple program execution Multiple operational environments
Application Software	Modular programs/structured techniques High level languages
Management	Multiple locations/dissimilar operations Remote control

Table 2.1: Systems Technology Sophistication

Harris & Katz (1991) calculated different ratios, one being the *operating cost efficiency ratio* (OPEX) which is the ratio of total operating expense to income (turnover). The organisation with the largest OPEX ratio represents the least profitable organisation and the organisation with the smallest, the most profitable. Another ratio is called the *information technology expense ratio* (ITEX) and it is the ratio of IT expenses to non-interest operating expenses. The last ratio is called the *information technology cost efficiency ratio* (ITCE) and is the cost of information processing to sales revenue (turnover).

Using these formulae, they tracked IT investment against non-interest operating expenses. The results suggest that top performers, were more likely to spend a significantly higher proportion of their non-interest operating expense on IT, while the least profitable firms were more likely to spend a significantly smaller proportion of their non-interest operating expense on IT. They note, however, that each business situation should be evaluated on its own merits and thus could not provide an instrument guaranteed as universally reliable.

The findings of Harris & Katz (1991) showed that process integration was associated with reduced organisational costs. Higher levels of process integration may nullify some negative aspect of environmental uncertainty. They suggested that research into process restructuring needs a concentrated effort to identify the most relevant measures and develop a theory that will facilitate the selection of the appropriate measures for managerial control and decision making.

Economic characteristics of IT

The issue of IT investment research is receiving increased attention because of the role that IT plays in the strategic thinking of most large organisations. IT researchers should turn to economics as a reference discipline to help solve problems that managers have with IT investment because of the following economic characteristics of IT: supply (IS typically requires large capital investments); demand (benefits should be realised by users); investors in IT face uncertainty regarding the benefits of the IT; IS can impose significant costs on participants; and there could be savings on the cost of information in organisations and markets.

The following economic theories could be used to investigate IT investment (Bakos & Kemerer, 1990):

- *Information economics*: IS research can focus on the role of IS in determining the attributes and value of the information available to the decision-maker.

- *Economics of IT supply and demand*: In this area, researchers attempt to study the characteristics of IT production functions and IT cost functions in terms of trends, capabilities, and projections.

- *Economics of IT*. The economic evaluation of these tools.

- *IT and organisational performance*. Any organisation can use IT to obtain competitive advantage through efficiency.

- *Industrial organisation*. This refers to business behaviour and its implications.

Another aspect is the study of the comparative economics of organisations. This includes transaction cost theory and agency theory that focus on the nature of the relationship between multiple parties. Economics could also be used to quantify impacts of IT investments on productivity.

IT researchers should seek to identify areas of economic theory related to the economic characteristics of IT listed, i.e., scale, externalities, uncertainty, switching costs and information costs. It is these characteristics which drive much of the reasoning behind IT investment and should guide theory selection.

Quantifying the business value of IT

Carlson & McNurlin (1992) note that, with the growing importance of IT investment, calls have been made for methods of quantifying the benefits of these investments. Few organisations take systematic before and after measurements of IT investments and even fewer relate IT benefits to business performance. Basic principles were presented for measuring IT investment which were reworked and combined with the work of other authors as a working guide for IT managers.

Carlson & McNurlin (1992) created a *functional quality index* by asking users whether the application of IT provided the appropriate functions, if the data was reliable, and so forth. The *technical quality index* was derived by asking questions of the maintenance staff (Howard Rubin Associates *cited* by Carlson & McNurlin, 1992). By reviewing the complete portfolio of IT applications, functional managers can better evaluate the risks of remaining on an obsolete technical platform as well as decide what to do with systems that do not meet users' needs. Carlson & McNurlin (1992) called attention to the demands of top managers for quantitative measurements of the value their organisations received from their IT investments.

They claim that nearly every large organisation has some sort of measurement in place, each developed through its own, homegrown methodology. Most of the organisations' measurements were tied solely to the managers of the I/S operation. Carlson & McNurlin (1992) state that:

the last three years have seen an almost explosive effort to help top executives understand where payoffs are coming from IT investments.

They cited reasons for the increased interest as including new working relationships between business managers and IS departments as a result of corporate quality programmes and an increased involvement in outsourcing.

Carlson & McNurlin (1992) claim that top managers are giving measurement increased attention and that IS managers need to respond by understanding how to quantify IS value. There are some guiding measurement principles like: credibility starts with proven information systems department efficiency; business and technology factors need to be integrated; both business performance and quality need to be measured; no single measure is available; executives must be educated; total quality management (TQM) requires a strong IS department; models now exist; bench marking is essential; poor systems quality hurts business performance; and asset accounting is essential. Carlson & McNurlin 1992) argue that:

anyone trying to give top managers an accurate picture of what they are getting (or can get) from IT investments should pay special attention to these principles.

Carlson & McNurlin (1992) claim that there is no correlation between IS effectiveness and corporate performance. However, researchers who have looked into the details have been able to uncover correlations. Business units that minimise IT costs do so by centralising their IS functions and they do not categorise IS functions with clients. Systems departments that maximise effectiveness, on the other hand, have a 50-50 split in their reporting structure. Half the functions report up the IS hierarchy while the other half report to business units. Lodahl & Reditt (*cited* by Carlson & McNurlin, 1992) claim that they have uncovered two predictors of IS effectiveness: organisations with a formal, written plan were less effective than those without one, while those which integrated the activities of the IS and business units during planning were the most effective. The planning process, not formal policy, predicts IS effectiveness.

While most hardware expenditure is treated as investments, software and people are not, yet these two resources are the most valuable assets. Some experts are now calling expenditure and the introduction of business change to be treated as investments and ongoing operations to be treated as expenses. Keen, *cited* by Carlson & McNurlin (1992), believes that all expenditure for

IS infrastructures (hardware, software, or people) should be treated as investments. Treating them as expenses creates an unrealistic expectation of immediate payoff. Carlson & McNurlin (1992) state that:

unfortunately, IS departments are required to allocate costs in such a way that they recover costs invested. That needs to change. IT should be managed as a capital asset, Keen and others are saying now.

Cotten & Hogbin (1995) believe that managing a project is enough of a challenge. They note that business value engineering addresses the gap between established and practical techniques of managing quality, risks and costs and managing the benefits of a project through realisation. They argue that principles of business value engineering are already practised by leading users of IT to ensure that the value of the investment is realised. They note that there are well-established and practical techniques to manage quality, risk and costs, but techniques to manage the benefits of a project through to realisation, are less well defined. Cotten & Hogbin (1995) observed that not all-organisational teams set out to identify benefits from a secure base, thus jeopardising the process of benefits identification.

Cotten & Hogbin (1995) developed a system called business value engineering (BVE), describing some processes as part of it. These are: get the right sponsor and benefits evaluation team; establish a credit Value Linkage Diagram which shows the IT and non-IT enablers; integrate business activities into the project plan; and ensure individual accountability for benefits delivery. Some of the strengths of BVE are: it provides a robust and comprehensive framework within which to identify and manage the expected benefits from an investment project; it comprises the total project and not simply technological solutions; it is a fundamental and proven method; and it can be applied to projects which will have both hard and soft benefits.

Evaluation of IT

Esther & Brooke (1995) have attempted to formulate a more holistic model for the evaluation of IT investments than existing methodologies, one that balances qualitative with quantitative criteria. Their model focuses on details of structure rather than content as they believe that the latter should be decided according to its context rather than prescribed. They believe that the apparent lack of success of previous models in evaluating IT investment is due to a poor understanding of the impacts of IT as a resource and the consequent absence of appropriate measures for assessing the total effects of IT. Better management can only come through an improved understanding of the concepts of both IT and of value in the widest business sense. The problem is the lack of understanding about the concept of evaluation itself. Esther & Brooke (1995) note that:

despite the availability of sophisticated estimation tools, and the use of prototyping, the determination of even tangible costs such as developmental costs for major applications remains both difficult and unreliable.

Esther & Brooke (1995) claim that there are two principal sources of risk which are often not fully incorporated into the evaluation process. One is that if the implementation is less than smooth, the extra implementation time contributes to excess costs. The second is that some risks are associated with data security. Some benefits are difficult to achieve or measure because they are intangible. IT investment is a component of wider organisational change. Attributing an accurate portion of benefits to the IT component can be problematic.

IT has many stakeholders - business users, government, manufacturers, customers/suppliers, competitors, and employees. It also has a high profile within the financial services industry (e.g., banks, insurance companies, etc.). Various reasons for the lack of visible benefits have been suggested by these stakeholders. Some are: outdated and ineffective evaluation methodologies; the time lag between the introduction of IT and its impact; the substantial proportion of benefits which are passed on to customers in the form of improved service quality; and technological determinism and the tendency to surrender important IT investment decisions to IT specialists.

Some methodologies argue that technological determinism has resulted in a sub-optimisation of IT investments. Esther & Brooke (1995) selected some methodologies that differed from the usual ones used and analysed in order to compare a broad cross-section of current approaches, ranging from the traditional to the more progressive approaches. These methodologies were:

traditional cost-benefit analysis; Kester's growth options model; risk analysis; balanced scorecard; information economics; and business ranking method. They came to the conclusion that:

the logic of the existing methodology range from totally intangible faith or gut feel to hard financial benefits.

Esther & Brooke (1995) also conducted interviews, the results suggesting the following guidelines for designing an IT evaluation strategy: choose a business strategy; identify domains needing performance improvement; identify critical success factors (CSFs) for each domain; assess anticipated benefits for any IT project against these CSFs; attribute a relative weighting to each domain and corresponding CSFs; conduct a *post ante* review of actual against expected benefits; and keep in mind existing methodologies rarely differentiate between costs and risks; the need to adopt multiple evaluation criteria; form joint user/IT specialist teams to explore IT project feasibility; let projects be owned by line managers who should be accountable for them; and make value a function of risks, costs and benefits. Esther & Brooke (1995) perceive a valuable system as one in which benefits outweigh costs and minimised risks. They called their eventual model the *Business-Wide Value Model* (BWVM).

According to Esther & Brooke (1995) the process must be led by the strategy of business. They note that:

in business terms, a project becomes valuable when it provides the organisation with the opportunity to realise its chosen objectives.

They note that the identification of CSFs require discussion at all levels and should involve those who eventually have to participate in data collection and evaluation. These discussions can be followed by the idea that stakeholders form joint committees to discuss projects before they are presented to senior managers.

Esther & Brooke (1995) claim that the overall impact and value of an IT investment should involve an aggregation of the anticipated effects in the areas the IT investment is placed. The stage of horizontal weighting determines the relative priorities attached to each domain for improvement and should be linked to the motivation for undertaking the project. There are six reasons: must do; strategic; efficiency; effectiveness; research; and nice to have. The total value of the project is thus the sum of the weighted scores obtained in each domain. This score can only be determined after consideration of the total score from each domain. According to Esther & Brooke (1995):

within each domain the organisation must establish the extent to which the project is aligned to each consolidated CSF. A large positive score represents strong alignment, whereas a negative score indicates a mismatch.

Esther & Brooke (1995) believe that the model shares some features with existing methodologies and that the BWVM combines different ideas and approaches into a single and explicit framework. As none of those questioned have faulted the model's logic, it is believed that it has potential for influencing future approaches to IT evaluation. The model should be valuable to organisations with the capability to formulate a business vision leading to specific objectives and CSFs. For non-IT investments, the same logic can be applied, although the choice of relevant domains should be based on the nature of the resource under consideration. They claim that their model can help managers make more self-aware and consistent decisions.

Farbey *et al.* (1995a, 1995b) note that, in response to the need for evaluation of IT investment, many methods for carrying out an IS investment evaluation have been developed. In practice, they discovered that most organisations use some form of Return on Investment calculation, supplemented by a description of intangible and strategic benefits. However, to choose an appropriate method it is necessary to understand: the assumptions that underlie the method; the nature of the system; and the nature of the context into which the system is introduced. In an earlier paper, Farbey *et al.* (1992) proposed a method for matching the above, based on a series of 2x2 matrices describing system and context.

They used some organisations that had recently installed information systems and looked specifically at the procedures and methods they employed in evaluating the new system. Virtually half the systems had been installed as acts of faith. They devised a series of questions aimed at capturing the relevant characteristics. These questions were derived empirically by abstracting from research interviews with the organisations and from literature. They were grouped into questions about the system, organisation and the external circumstances surrounding the investment.

Farbey et al. (1995b) note that:

superimposing the individual matrices onto a summary matrix gave a rough impression as to the nature of the product. The summary project showed two contrasting set of questions: one, the vertical axis, subsumed the questions on the evaluation constraints - were they well defined or fuzzy? The other, horizontal axis, reflected the role of IT - was this a radical application, or an essentially conservative one? The methods were similarly classified so that by comparing the two it was possible to suggest which method, or group of methods might be the most promising.

A series of issues were derived from the use of the matrices on the empirical side. These were that: the contingencies are themselves unstable; as projects progress, they move through the boxes; the perception of the project situation may vary from one stakeholder group to another; the IT department may be more aware of the technical complexity of a problem and classify it as box 2 (Figure 2.1) while the business users will be more aware of goal conflict and classify it as box 4; organisations may act to manage risk. For example, a radical application of IT may be programmed in COBOL or an application may be leading edge with respect to the technology, but organisationally quite routine. Or a project may be deliberately pitched so that the bulk of it is conservative, but some special features are radical and innovative so that overall, the risk is contained.

Role of IT	***Conservative***	***Radical***
Evaluation constraints	Tactical	Strategic
	Quantifiable	Qualitative
	Simple	Sophisticated
	Support Systems	Core system
	Follower	Leader
	Certain impact	Uncertain impact

Well defined: Specification stage Standard decision procedure Numbers important Specific application Stable environment		
Direct Impact		
Fuzzy: Requirement stage Ad hoc procedure Numbers not important Infrastructure Turbulent environment Indirect impact		

Figure 2.1: The Farbey et al. (1995b) matrix

Farbey *et al.* (1995b) note that to:

relate the empirical work to the theoretical analysis has enabled a better understanding of why the empirical classification worked and what further questions could or should be asked. In other words, the work is properly grounded in a recognised theoretical framework of ideas. Also, the classification can be seen to centre on two groups of questions. The first is about goals, objectives, constraints, ends. The second is about cause and effect, how well known the relationships are, how clearly the means can be seen to effect the ends. It is a question about what is probable.

Some authors (Peters, 1990; Esther & Brooke, 1995) developed an evaluation methodology for IT investments. However, each model used a different approach that each author believes are the correct one. Harris & Katz (1991) also found that high performers were likely to spend a larger ratio of their non-interest operating expenses on IT in the same industry.

Economic theory can be used to try and assess IT investment and problems managers may have with IT investment. Carlson & McNurlin (1992) note that few organisations have a systematic before and after measurement of IT investments. The problem of risk as part of any IT investment was addressed by Esther & Brooke (1995) noting that it is not fully incorporated into the evaluation process. Some areas remain to open to discussion while none of the authors could argue with confidence that their model is the correct one, nor could they provide conclusive proof of the correctness of their models. Table 2.2 summarises the themes and issues covered by the authors discussed in this chapter.

Author	**Date**	**Theme**	**Journal**	**Important points**
Ahituv & Neumann	1990	IS management	Book	• economic criteria should include all costs • look at different cost elements
Butler-Cox Foundation	1990	Value from IT	Research Report	• no single measure for IT • judgement to be applied
Carlson & McNurlin	1992	Measuring IT	I/S analyser	• quantifying IT benefits • relate benefits to organisational performance
Clemons & Weber	1990	SISP	Journal of MIS	• difficult to justify IT • Benefits not easily measured
Cotten & Hogbin	1995	Value of IT	2nd Henley Conference	• problem of IT benefits - • IT benefit identification
Deitz & Renkema	1993	Justifying IT investments	2nd Henley Conference	• planning gap • CBA completed
Earl	1992	Justification of investments IT	Journal of IT	• IT oversold and under-delivered • IT can change business
Esther & Brooke	1995	Evaluating IT	2nd Henley Conference	• no measurement of total impact of IT • IT costs a problem
Farbey *et al*	1995	Evaluating IT	2nd Henley investments	• use ROI Conference
Glazer	1993	Value of IT	IBM Systems Journal	• full potential of IT not realised • should concentrate on information
Harris & Katz	1991	IT intensity	Organisation Science	• develop CBA hierarchy • should use IT to better organisation

Author	Date	Theme	Journal	Important points
Kaye *et al.*	1995	Hidden investment in IT	2nd Henley Conference	• IT has changed some organisations • IT is in a continuum
Katz	1993	Measuring IT's business value	Journal of ISM	• prove benefits • no relationship between IT and performance
Lubbe	1994	IT investment	M-dissertation	• some models for IT investment measurement
Mukhopadhyay *et al.*	1995	IT benefits	2nd Henley Conference	• problem - impact of IT • analysis of cost & benefit
Peters	1990	Benefits of IT	Journal of IT	• CBA hierarchy • own methodology
Powell	1992	IT and other investments	Journal of IT	• competitive advantage • classification scheme
Tam	1992	IT and capital budgeting	Information & Management	• capital budgeting has little impact • problem with costs estimation
Ward *et al.*	1995	IT benefits	2nd Henley Conference	• methodologies not satisfactory • benefits not always realised

Table 2.2 A summary of authors discussed in the chapter

Critical review of key studies described above

From the above review, it is clear that there is a considerable amount of activity in the field of information systems evaluation research. However, these papers reveal that thinking in this area of study is fairly fragmented with there being many different approaches and no one attempting to provide any real type of integration. Work in this field is conducted at many major universities and practices all over the world. However, there has yet not been any outstanding theorist who has managed to integrate all this varied and fragmented thinking. The issues would therefore be kept in mind when the research is conducted.

There is really little or no sequence in the models and theories provided by this research. Unlike other social sciences there is no John Maynard Keynes,

Max Webber or Karl Marx. Even the best known authors in the field of information systems cannot be considered to have developed any *grand theory*. Furthermore, most of the studies were fragmented in their approach, i.e. they look at a single issue from a single angle. There is little or no attempt to acquire a holistic view of information technology evaluation. This means that it is not possible to use an established theory as the basis for this book and that it has been necessary to adopt a grounded theory approach, which will be described in Chapter 3.

In addition, the research described in this chapter is overwhelmingly positivist in its methodological approach. Phenomenological or interpretative research is almost entirely absent. It is increasingly believed that a positivist research paradigm alone does not provide the answers which are required in business and management studies. Furthermore, the studies described generally do not debate in any detail the cause and effect situation which is clearly an important issue in understanding the intricate relations involved in making an information system a success.

Additionally these research studies have not looked at the business processes in depth, or at the business system (organisation) as a whole. They could have used a holistic approach, with IT as one of the sub-systems in the organisation. The academics did not approach the research with an open mind, but rather tested set academic rules before conducting the research.

For most of the 1960s, 1970s and early 1980s, executives largely ignored the issue of the returns their IT investments gave their organisations. It was generally believed that outlays for hardware and software quickly paid for them as IS automated basic functions such as accounting, inventory control and payroll. However, as the 1980's progressed and IT expenses increased, many executives were hard put to find any measurable productivity gains as a result of their outlay in IT. The large amounts of funds expended were justified by arguing that IT investments directly supported the organisation's business strategy.

Of course, IT has an effect on business strategy and at the same time business strategy should have an effect on IT. But to obtain strategic advantage IT action programmes should be devised and targets set. In South Africa, however, there is a tendency to shift resources to meet contingencies.

In the literature review, authors noted that some of the key concerns expressed by IT executives are that they need to keep abreast with new technology and systems, and that they need solid business orientation and strong organisational skills to manage the expanding role of their function successfully. However, they do not always have the time to achieve this and have to rely on their staff. The point of departure noticed in the literature shows that technological change will have a significant effect on the user. Furthermore, these changes will affect the IT infrastructure and applications which are a cause of concern for management. Investment appraisal and benefits realisation should be an important and integral part of IT investments. The literature inspected does not place enough emphasis on the productivity aspect of IT.

Authors argued in the literature review that IT managers need to concentrate on improving business productivity, quality and competitiveness. However, the critical challenge facing the IT function is to keep their costs under control. Some authors also claim that technology also changes internal business processes and this is a process that organisations could utilise. It can also be claimed that a new understanding of the impacts of IT investment in the organisation could be a problem, but this problem could be overcome if a holistic approach to systems is used. New technology is usually the springboard for changes designed to meet organisational needs better and quicker.

The author believe that IT efforts (budgets, equipment and human resources) are often misplaced and this leaves the IT department with little time to respond to requests from users for new applications. Too much emphasis is placed upon economic criteria - executives should look into all aspects in a holistic way. This is because IT is part of an overall system and benefits should be selected without trying to determine how to measure each one separately.

Words alone are not enough to execute an IT strategy, it must also be financed and if the organisation's management is smart, they should insist that all of an organisation's IS expenditure yields explicit and measurable economic benefits over the lifetime of the project. This is where most of the authors differs, the business benefits of any significant IT project can be determined through information value analysis. Such a process can evaluate whether the changes in business practices that result from an IT investment justify the expense. Organisations should also conduct systems analysis regularly, measuring the worth of all IT projects, past and present, which form their current information-processing infrastructure.

Organisations could select projects likely to have the highest impact on the organisation, and allocate resources to this project. IT departments have problems delivering projects on time, within budget and at levels needed in the organisation. The IT policy of organisations may lack the provision to capture the advantages of IT investment by linking IT support to business change. Without management's perseverance, the potential of IT to change the organisation for the better will rarely be realised.

It was also noted in the literature that certain areas remain open to discussion and that many models exist that can measure IT investment and the benefits to be derived from an IT investment. Attempts were made, for example, to quantify benefits from IT investment, but no definite conclusion could be drawn (see 2.3). It can be argued that no concrete calculation of the total impact of IT had been made; it can be suggested that most surveys underestimate total investment in IT. There is thus a need for the creation of a formal model to evaluate IT investments. The element of associated risk is also ignored by most of the literature.

Research questions

The above literature review and the critique thereof lead directly to the fundamental objective of this book which is to investigate the application in practice, and the effectiveness of evaluation of IT investment measurements in organisations in a developing country, and also to investigate the performance of IT investments in the same organisations. Thus the following research questions were identified: (i) How do managers identify and evaluate IT investment and IT benefits?; (ii) What is involved in implementing sound

IT investments?; (iii) Would other organisations agree that this is good practice?; and (iv) Is it possible to develop the theory into managerial guidelines?

CONCLUSION

This chapter refers to attempts by researchers (Deitz & Renkema (1995), Mukhopadhyay *et al.* (1995) and Harris & Katz (1991) to quantify benefits received from IT investment. All these authors note that no concrete calculation of the total impact of IT has been made. However, some studies in recent literature kept the concept of the change in risk in mind while investing resources in IT. Authors like Harris & Katz (1991) noted the importance of risk when making an IT investment.

Over the last few years, some authors (Clemons & Weber, 1990) have examined the possibility of quantifying IT expenditure. Farbey *et al.* (1995b) suggest that most surveys underestimate the total investment in IT. Some authors (Harris & Katz, 1991) note that the link between IT and performance varies. The problem is the measurement of the intangible benefits of IT. They all agree, however, that the value of information should be closely linked to the decision supported by the information available. Ahituv & Neumann (1990) claim that all the components of IT should be considered if the right pricing method for the charge back of IT is to be selected.

Some authors (Harris & Katz, 1991) established a definite link between IT investment and an increasing profitability margin. They note that an increase in the profitability margin could be found in similar organisations in the same industry. All the studies researched agree that investing in IT could make a contribution towards the benefits that the organisation receives.

As can be seen from the above, a multiplicity of work has been carried out in the field of measuring the impact of IT investment on the profitability and risk of an organisation. Because researchers have investigated different perspectives and these credited experts have expressed different views, the author believes that a need exists for the creation of grounded theory which will make a useful contribution to managers in their attempts to obtain good results from the application of information systems.

ENDNOTES

[1] This book has focused largely on tangible benefits which have been defined by Remenyi et al. (1995) as those benefits which directly affect the bottom line of organisation, i.e., that can be translated into monetary terms. Because of the problems experienced with the translation of intangible benefits into monetary terms, they were either ignored or combined with tangible benefits.

[2] Tangible non-monetary costs are those that bring a visible benefit to the organisation, but are difficult to assign a specific value to it, i.e., how much of the increase in turnover is because of this IT investment?

REFERENCES

Ahituv N. & Neumann S.(1990). *Principles of Information Systems for Management*, Third Edition, WC Brown Publishers, Dubuque.

Bakos J.Y. & Kemerer C.F. (1992). "Recent applications of economic theory in Information Technology research," *Information Technology Research*, 3(5).

Butler-Cox Foundation (1990:). "Getting value from Information Technology", *Research Report 75*, June, London.

Carlson W. & McNurlin B. (1992). "Basic Principles For Measuring IT value," *I/S Analyzer*,30(10), 1 - 13.

Clemons E.K. & Row M.C. (1991)."Sustaining IT advantage: The role of structural differences," *MIS Quarterly*, September.

Clemons E.K. & Weber B.W. (1990). "Strategic Information Technology Investments: Guidelines for Decision Making", *Journal of Management Information Systems*, Fall 7(2), 9 - 28.

Cognitech Services (Lodahl T & Redditt I) *cited* by Carlson W. & McNurlin B. 1992 in "Basic Principles For Measuring IT value," *I/S Analyzer*,30(10), 1 - 13.

Cotten S. & Hogbin G. (1995). "Engineering the Value of IT", *Proceedings of the 2nd Henley Conference on the Evaluation of IT Investments*, Henley Management College, Henley, UK, 87 - 95.

Deitz R.M.H. & Renkema T.J.W. (1995). "Planning and justifying investments in Information Technology: A framework with case study illustrations", *Proceedings of the 2nd Henley Conference on the Evaluation of IT Investments*, Henley Management College, Henley, UK, 28 - 41.

Earl M.J. (1992)."Putting IT in its place: a polemic for the nineties", *Journal of Information Technology*, No 7, 100 - 108.

Esther J.A.K. & Brooke C. (1995)."A business value model for evaluating information technology investments", *Proceedings of the 2nd Henley Conference on the Evaluation of IT Investments*, Henley Management College, Henley, UK, 277 - 301.

Farbey B., Land F. & Targett D. (1993). *How to assess your IT investments: A study of methods and practice;* Butterworth Heinemann, London.

Farbey B., Land F. & Targett D. (1995a). "A taxonomy of information systems applications: the benefits' evaluation ladder," *European Journal of Information Systems*, No 4, 41 - 50.

Farbey B., Land F. & Targett D. (1995b). "System - Method - Context: a contribution towards the development of guidelines for choosing a method of evaluating I/S investment," *Proceedings of the 2nd Henley Conference on the Evaluation of IT Investments*, Henley Management College, Henley, UK, 267 - 276.

Glazer R. (1993). "Measuring the value of information: The Information intensive organisation," *IBM Systems Journal*, 32(1), 99 - 110.

Harris S.E. & Katz J.L. (1991). "Organisational Performance and Information Technology investment intensity in the insurance industry", *Organisation Science*, 2(3), 263 - 295.

Katz A.I. (1993). "Measuring Technology's Business Value: Organizations seek to prove IT benefits," *Information Systems Management*, Winter, 33 - 39.

Kaye G.R., Hinton C.M. & Armstrong S. (1995). "The Hidden Investment in IT: Dependency, Legacy and Heritage", *Proceedings of the 2nd Henley Conference on the Evaluation of IT Investments*, Henley Management College, Henley, UK, 249 - 259.

Keen P. *cited* by Carlson W. & McNurlin B. (1992) in "Basic Principles For Measuring IT value", *I/S Analyzer*, 30(10), 1 - 13.

Lubbe S.I. 1994: *The impact of Information Technology (IT) on the financial performance of organisations in a developing country*, M.Com.-Thesis, UCT, Cape Town.

Mukhopadhyay T., Kekre S. & Kalathur S. (1995). "Business value of Information Technology: A study of electronic data interchange," *MIS Quarterly*, June, 137 - 156.

Peters G. (1990). "Beyond strategy - benefits identification and management of specific IT investments," *Journal of Information Technology*, No 5, 205 - 214.

Powell P. (1992). "Information Technology Evaluation: Is it different?", *Journal of Operational Research Society*, 43(1), 29 - 42.

Remenyi D. Money A & Twite. A. (1995). *The effective management and measurement of IT costs and Benefits*, Butterworth-Heinman.

Remenyi D. & Williams B. (1995). Some aspects of methodology for research in information systems, *Journal of Information Systems*, No 10, 191 - 201

Sutherland F. (1993). *Evaluating Information Systems investments in South Africa*, A master's dissertation, University of the Witwatersrand, Johannesburg.

Tam K.Y. (1992). "Capital budgeting in information systems development", *Information & Management*, No 23, 345 - 357.

Ward J., Taylor P. & Bond P. (1995)."Identification, Realisation and Measurement of IT benefits," *2nd Henley Conference of the Evaluation of IT Investments*, Henley Management College, Henley, UK, 133 - 145.

Chapter Three

Research Methodology

An overview of the chapter

This chapter discusses the research methodology and the research philosophy which underpins this book.

Aim of the book

The aim of the book is to:

1. study and evaluate the approach by organisations to IT investment and IT benefit identification;

2. develop a preliminary theory of good practice in the field;

3. test this theory by reference to other enterprises and practitioners; and thereby,

4. to develop the theory into managerial guidelines.

Why this book is important

Although IT investment evaluation has only recently[1] become an important issue, interest in the area has grown over the last couple of years. It is clear from previous research (Butler-Cox Foundation,1990; Barua *et al.*, 1991) that many organisations are concerned about the issue of IT investment because they are requested to use the information resources effectively. This is in keeping with a general need to become more competitive (Daniels & Daniels, 1993; Daniels,1994). Thus, more and more organisations will attempt to establish, formulate and implement the IT investment that will meet their organisation's needs for efficiency and effectiveness (Earl, 1992; Farbey *et al.*,1992; 1993).

Much of the literature and the research reviewed by Lubbe (1994) focused on a calculation of the total impact of IT without commenting, or providing guidelines for managers who wish to make the IT investment which would best fit into their present jigsaw of IT investments.

It is, of course, not easy to identify IT investments that will support organisational strategies and to establish a method as to how organisations can do this is of practical value to managers. Similarly, the selection of IT investments requires detail and advice as to how it can be helpful to managers. Conducting research into practical formulation and selection issues, as well as its eventual effect on organisational performance, is an important issue that demands attention. Therefore the book will study managerial mechanisms within the organisation that affect IT investment as well as its evaluation.

The nature of a methodology

A scientific methodology should form the basis of any book which claims to add something of value to the body of knowledge. Chadwick *et al.* (1984) describes scientific methodology as a systematic observation of nature. Einstein (1950) argues that:

... The object of all science, whether natural science or psychology, is to co-ordinate our experiences into a logical system.

Einstein (1922) defined science as:

.. The attempt to make the chaotic diversity of our sense - experience correspond to a logically uniform system of thought. In this system, single experiences must be correlated with the theoretical structure in such a way that the resulting coordination is unique and convincing.

Chadwick *et al.* (1984) define method as a way of assessing the validity of ideas about reality and existence through systematic study and observation, together with the recording of observations and how they were obtained so that the resulting factors may be checked and modified by others. Smith (1990) notes that knowing how to use the tools and techniques of research does not in itself guarantee the effectiveness of any person in carrying out a scientific investigation. Remenyi *et al.* (1996) state that science is just one human way of looking at the world of reality. This way of thinking suggests that science interprets and not necessarily in a neutral way. However, scientific theories are open to endless revision and current scientific ideas are nothing more than human work in progress. Remenyi (1996) states that scientific methodology is a system of explicit rules and procedures upon which claims of knowledge as a result of the research are evaluated.

Methodologies are neither closed nor infallible and Lee (1989) points out that:

..Scientists have not yet settled among themselves on a single method of what science is, let alone how it should be researched.

Scientific understanding proceeds by way of constructing and analysing models of the segments or aspects of reality under study. The purpose of these models is not to give a mirror image of reality, not to include all its elements in their exact sizes and proportions, but rather to single out and make available for intensive investigation those elements which are decisive (Baran & Sweezy, 1970). Lee (1989) noted that it was argued that no field can potentially be a science unless its theories are cast according to a demarcation criterion.

A methodology may serve as a set of rules for reasoning whereby evaluation of facts can be used to draw inferences. Haug (1996) noted that the field of evaluation is not static. Remenyi (1990) notes that the use of a methodology infers some competence in logical reasoning. The researcher might be able to establish or verify some theories and must be validated by some form of empirical evidence. Therefore, primary benefits of a scientific methodology are that:

1. It facilitates communication between scientists, allowing them to share experiences. It also makes replication of the research easier. Replication of research is always necessary to safeguard against unintentional errors as well as deception or fraud.

2. It ensures that an acceptable logical structure is being used. Scientific research requires both empirical observation and valid logical reasoning. The methodology is an articulation of valid logical reasoning. The rules of classification, definition, deduction, and indirect sampling, if used, must be articulated in the methodology.

3. It institutionalises conceptual frameworks for communication, rules of reasoning, procedures and methods for observance and verification. Methodology demands conformity. However, care must be taken that methodology does not hinder new discoveries and, by implication, scientific progress (Nachmias & Nachmias: 1989).

Methodology is an issue facing the social scientist in conducting research in that it provides a basis on which the researcher may assert the validity of his/ her findings. Scientific knowledge, according to Remenyi (1990), is knowledge provable by both reason and observance and methodology must address both issues in terms of logic validity and empirical verification. These two criteria are translated into a research process.

Initial stages of the research

The theoretical and philosophical basis of this book is empirical research. The research strategy employed was based of the approach described by (Remenyi and Williams 1995) and is shown in Figure 3.1.

A literature survey of IT investment and evaluation issues (Chapter 2) was completed. This was completed in two stages. After the preliminary stage, the literature review was written up and became the basis of the research proposal which was validated by presentation to the research committee and accepted by the University. Subsequently the literature review was extended and a critique was developed and research questions were established.

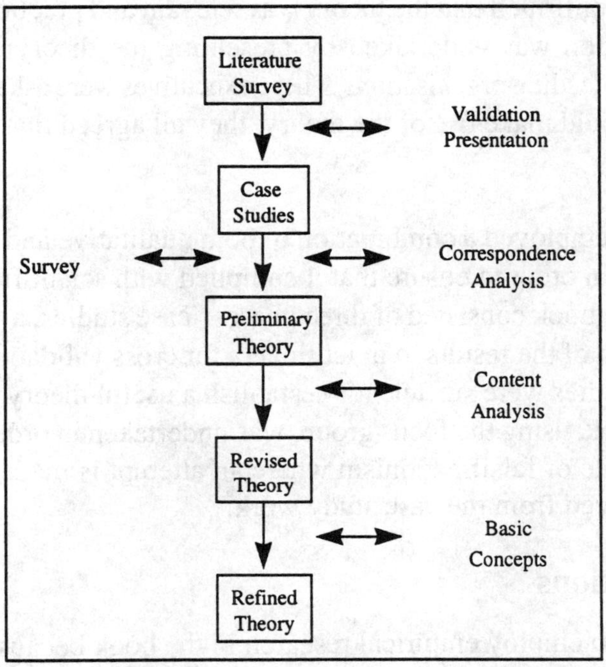

Figure 3.1: Derived from - The research process (Remenyi & Williams (1993))

As there is no appropriate grand theory from which to derive hypotheses it was decided to use a grounded theory approach and to collect evidence through the use of case studies. The author then conducted a series of case studies (Chapter 4) which were used to develop a theory or theoretical conjecture concerning the formulation, adaptation and implementation of an IT investment and its benefits. It was decided to use case studies because the focus of the book was to understand the *how* and *why* of a phenomena of IT investment and its evaluation within the organisational context.

The evidence collected through the empirical case study research resulted in a large transcript which was analysed using both content and correspondence analysis and thus developed into a grounded theoretical conjecture. The grounded theory was cross validated by discussion with a focus group consisting of IT managers.

The managers confirmed that the theory was relevant and practical. A second level of validation was undertaken by presenting the theory to senior IT executives from leading organisations. These executives were asked to confirm whether they could make use of the theory; they all agreed that this was the case.

Thus, the book employed a combination of both qualitative and quantitative methodologies in order to ensure that it complied with scientific principles. In summary, the book consisted of three phases: case studies, a focus group, and presentation of the results to practitioners for cross validation purposes. Twenty case studies were sufficient to establish a useful theory. The second phase of the book, using the focus group, was undertaken in order to comply with the principle of falsificationism where an attempt is made to disprove the theory deduced from the case study work.

Research options

It was decided to employ empirical research in the book because it enabled the researcher to get close to the organisation, gaining insight at the same time into the situations that exist around IT investment and investment identification. Empirical research also helped the book to consider the meaning of certain more or less naturally occurring phenomena in the world of IT investment (Easterby-Smith *et al*, 1993). The empirical approach is also particularly useful, where relations between things are contingent, and thus should be answered by observing actual cases (Sayer, 1993).

On the other hand, the book also has a theoretical underpinning from the literature review. This was the result of the study of the research area through the writings of others and through discourse with learned or informed individuals, such as the various informants. The theory produced here was the result of reflections on the ideas supplied by more than 70 individuals consulted during the tenure of the book.

Bias in research

On the issue of bias, it is naive to assert that any form of research, or perhaps human activity generally, is without bias. Even in the physical and life sciences the researchers' bias is reflected in the subject researched, the experiments chosen, as well as the way the experiment is conducted. Thus bias cannot be totally eliminated but should be recognised and its implications accepted i.e. lived with.

Sub-conscience bias on the part of the researcher is a problem. Of course, triangulation may be used to help in this respect, but in the final analysis, an argument based on a judgement is always required in research (Collins, 1994). This may not be easy to make with personal prejudices playing an overtly influential and important role. The bias problem has been well described by Hubbard (1979) when she said:

The mythology of science asserts that with many different scientists all asking their own questions and evaluating the answers independently, whatever personal bias creeps into their individual answers is cancelled out when the large picture is put together. This might conceivably be so if scientists were women and men from all sorts of different cultural and social backgrounds who came to science with very different ideologies and interests. But since, in fact, they have been predominantly university-trained white males from privileged social backgrounds, the bias has been narrow and the product often reveals more about the investigator than about the subject being researched.

With regard to research findings, it is important that these are honestly presented and not produced in such a way as to simply support the opinions or prejudices of the researcher. This is indeed hard to accomplish. Ideally the researcher is trying to apply "disinterested intellectual curiosity" (Trevelyan, 1942), but this is almost impossible as was pointed out by Gould (1980) when he said:

Science is not an objective, truth-directed machine, but a quintessentially human activity, affected by passion, hopes, and cultural biases. Cultural traditions of thought strongly influence scientific theories.

Sometimes, if not frequently, personal bias is so subtle that the researcher is not even aware of it. In fact, many would argue that a researcher should not attempt to compensate for this bias, but should simply state clearly the possible biases involved and allow the readers to compensate for these themselves.

Case studies as research strategy

The case study methodology's approach to gathering data with which to develop grounded theory was selected for several reasons. This will become clear from the description below of the case study's methodology.

The term *case study* refers to two entirely different issues. As a teaching-learning device, it is a highly effective end well-established technique for use in the classroom to simulate real-life situations. The way to handle case studies is similar to the way business issues are mostly handled. The classroom and the syndicate groups provide the simulated business meetings in which the participant can learn both the skills of listening and presenting a point of view. The environment in which the case study is used helps participants to develop a degree of confidence in their judgment, as well as a degree of humility (Edge & Coleman, 1986).

Definition of a case study as a teaching-learning device

From a teaching-learning point of view, a case study may be defined as a technique for presenting ideas or data primarily for the purposes of simulating discussion and debate. Case studies may address any subject area and may range from single page documents to lengthy tomes. It is one of the oldest ways of presenting information, with its roots reaching back to times when myths and fables were used as teaching devices (Remenyi, 1990). The fact that the circumstances portrayed in these situations were fictitious did not in any way detract from their use as learning material. Thus, in general, a teaching-learning case study need not reflect a complete or accurate rendition of a real-life situation as its purpose is simply to present a framework for discussion and debate. From the case writer's point of view, the main attribute of teaching-learning case studies is that they are written in such a way that they will stimulate readers to identify problems and seek solutions.

Definition of a case study as a research methodology

As a research strategy, it is a technique for answering *who*, *why* and *how* questions. The use of multiple evidence allows the researcher to provide a convincing argument as an answer to the questions. It is not essential to the validity of the case study research method that a case study should be able to be generalised. In this research, generalisation is not a central issue. The relevance of a case study is more important than its generality. When a case study is carried out systematically , critically and aimed at the improvement of understanding, then it is relevant. If any publication of its findings extends or expands the boundaries of existing knowledge of the subject area, then it is a valid form of research. As the case study methodology can produce excellent results on the hands of a skilled investigator, its use is on the rise in most areas of the social sciences and certainly in information research.

Stake (1994) identifies three types of studies using the case study method. In the first, he identifies intrinsic case studies in which the study is undertaken because the researcher wants a better understanding of the particular case. Using the instrumental case study as the second example, a particular instance is examined to provide insight into an issue or refinement of theory. In the third example, he used the term collective case study. In these, researchers may jointly study a number of case studies in order to inquire into the phenomenon, population, or general condition. The importance of it is that case studies are frequently discussed and analysed, and subsequently, courses of action are agreed upon in groups.

From a research strategy point of view, the case study methodology is a way of establishing valid and reliable information or research findings which add to the accumulated knowledge of the processes by which business and many other organisations' functions. It is a research strategy for the social scientist in the same sense as experiments are a research strategy for the natural scientist. Yin (1994) defines a case study as:

A case study from a research strategy point of view may be defined as an empirical inquiry that investigates a contemporary phenomenon within its real life context, when the boundaries between phenomenon and the context are not clearly evident, and in which the multiple source of evidence are used. It is particularly valuable in answering who, why and how questions in management research.

According to Bell (1987), the case study methodology has also been described as an umbrella term for a group of research methods which have in common the decision to focus an inquiry around a specific instance or event. The philosophy behind the case study is that sometimes just by looking carefully at a practical, real life instance, a full picture can be obtained of the actual interaction of variables or events. The case study allows the investigator to concentrate on specific instances in an attempt to identify interactive processes that may be crucial, but which are transparent to the large scale survey. Thus, the aim of the case study is to provide a three dimensional picture of the situation. It should illustrate relationships, corporate-political issues and patterns of influence within a particular context.

Case studies are being used to a larger extent by social science as both a research and a teaching vehicle, and especially in IS research (Lee, 1989). The scope of the case study is extensive, ranging from individuals, to organisational groups, to national policies or events. Cases are either persistent original (Stake, 1994), or one-of-a-kind situation. Cases are compared and their characteristics are studied and behaviour patterns noted. It is important to bear in mind that, despite explicit clarity, most cases are aggregates of complex behaviour (Stake, 1994). From a research point of view, the case study methodology describes the total situation as a combination of different factors. The case study focus on the description of the process or sequence of events in which the behaviour occurs, the study of individual or group behaviour in its total social setting, and the comparison of cases leading to the formulation of hypotheses as claimed by Stake (1994).

By means of the case study method it is possible to establish the number and variety of properties, qualities and habits combined in a particular instance. The depth of the inquiry possible through the case study method is significantly greater than any other research method such as a survey (Galliers, 1991). For example, although attempts are made to ascertain attitudes by means of questionnaires, the results are sometimes unsatisfactory as one cannot do justice to an attitude by ticking yes or no, or rating 1 to 5. The case study can go much further than this superficial analysis and can discuss greater variations and reasons for attitudes (e.g., if a respondent is asked to rate a service rendered in a case study context, he or she may reply with both a score on a preset scale and a list of explanations and/or caveats qualifying the score). The additional information is beneficial to the researcher who may use it either as explanatory notes to the findings produced from the questionnaire or as raw material for further content analysis.

Because the case study follows the logic of the experiment rather than logic of the survey, it is not necessary to repeat a case study many times (Yin, 1994). This is because the experiment starts with the formulation of a theory and then attempts to find evidence that will either support or disprove the theory while the survey attempts to get a general view of something. The experimental approach is used in the case study method of research. The reason why it is not necessary to repeat the experiment or case study many times, as is achieved with a survey, is the same as why it is not necessary to experiment with the boiling point of water many times to support or contradict the theory of transformation of liquids into gasses at a certain temperature. However, it is important to bear in mind that the case study methodology is not designed to measure the frequency of occurrence of events, but rather to support or reject theoretical propositions.

The different types of evidence on which a case study may be based

From a case study research strategy point of view, the case study methodology implies comprehensive and intensive study of the subject. Thoroughness is thus one of the first requisites. Facts must be ascertained from the enterprises or enterprises under study and then carefully interpreted. These may be obtained from documents, archives, interviews with any person who has knowledge of the subject, observations of the investigator, participant-observer interaction, as well as physical artifacts. This information must be weighed, tested and sifted to eliminate fictitious or false statements and where possible, personal opinions.

Bias in the case study

Case studies can rarely be objectively complete due to the bias of both the supplier and the recipient of the information. Stake (1994) regards this area of research as fraught with danger, primarily due to the problem of subjectivity interpreting data after it has been written down. Bias is everywhere, but can be minimised. It is the primary function of the researcher to minimise the bias level in which he is working. There are at least three obstacles in obtaining unbiased testimonials from observers:

1. The difficulties encountered by individuals in their being able to accurately remember.

2. The inhibitions individuals have in disclosing important feelings.

3. The suspicion individuals have about revealing information that might reflect poorly on them or their superiors.

However, the use of multiple sources of evidence can help substantially in improving the validity and reliability of the research. By studying every aspect of the problem from as many angles as possible, and by using various sources of evidence, the case study research strategy is a powerful research tool in the hands of a skilled investigator (Stake, 1994).

The significance of uniformity when recording data

In multiple case study research, where a series of cases is involved, uniformity of recording should be sought as it facilitates comparison between enterprises and situations which allows similarities and differences to be highlighted. Unless there is some uniformity of recording, it can be extremely difficult to recognise similarities and much of the usefulness of the case study method, as well as its scientific value, may be eliminated. The case study methodology presumes a well-defined problem with a clearly articulated hypothesis. This is part of case study design and it is necessary to have this aspect of the research firmly in place before any attempt is made to collect evidence or perform analysis.

The formality of the case study research methodology

The case study research methodology is often mistakenly thought to be rather informal (Stake: 1994). This because it is confused with case writing from a teaching-learning point of view. In fact, the case study research strategy methodology requires a distinctly formal approach. Before the research can approach, protocols must be drawn up. The protocol is a formal and detailed master plan for the research. It is a document in which full details of the case study research design, including details of the questions to be asked, field procedures for the researcher, details of all types of evidence required, as well as the structure of the final research must be specified.

The case study protocol

The case study protocol is both the instrument with which the case study is conducted, as well as the general rules and procedures with which the work is carried out. The protocol for this book is a primary tactic in increasing the reliability of the case study procedure and should have the following sections.

Objectives of the research

The main objective of the case study research is to obtain evidence as to how firms formulate and implement IT investment decisions and how to link IT investment to organisational performance. This will be achieved by using a series of unstructured interviews which will allow informants the opportunity of supplying information on a wide range of issues related to information, decision making, and implementation activities and organisational performance.

It is intended to allow the informants as much freedom in the interviews as possible as it is crucial to ensure that the interviewer does not in any way prejudge the evidence offered by them. Nonetheless, a list of discussion topics that the interviewer may use as an interview schedule has been developed. The topics are available to assist the interviewer if the discussion requires some prompting or guidance.

Key issues of the research

There are four key issues of this book:

1. to study and evaluate the approach by organisations to IT investment and IT benefit identification;
2. to develop a preliminary theory of good practice in the field;
3. to test this theory or theoretical conjecture by reference to other enterprises and practitioners; and
4. thereby develop the theory into managerial guidelines.

Interview schedule

1. How does the organisation categorise Information Technology?
2. What architecture does the hardware consist of?

3. Does top management agree with the definition and compilation of the IT in the organisation?

4. Has the IT investment decision been tied to any other investment decisions?

5. Have IT investment projects been carefully planned and have these investment projects been documented in specific detail including cost-benefit or other types of financial analysis?

6. Have these investment projects been thoroughly discussed with potential users before doing the investment?

7. Is there a policy decision to centralise/decentralise IT in the organisation (including control of the IT)?

8. Have IT investments been coordinated with other interfacing functions?

9. Have operators and managers received appropriated training?

10. Does the IT Department have greater freedom to respond to exceptions when they occur while doing the IT investment?

11. How do they determine whether IT investment has an effect on organisational performance?

Figure 3.2: Research objectives and interview schedules

The case study protocol

The overview include the objectives or issues on which the case study investigator should focus. Figure 3.2 displays the overview, as well as the interview schedule used to collect data during the unstructured case study interviews.

Field procedure reminders, etc.

The investigator has to work in the real world and thus cope with real world situations during the data collection plan, including the possibility of the respondent dropping out of the experiment or case study. Similarly, corporate documents may not always be available. Field procedures need to emphasize issues such as:

- defining who should be interviewed;
- gaining access to the right people;
- having adequate resources available such as time, paper, tape records, etc.;
- developing a procedure for discussing the research with other researchers; and
- making a schedule of the required data collection activities providing contingencies.

Figure 3.3 displays the protocol for the field procedures the author believes should be followed to conduct the case studies.

Case study protocols

At the center of the protocol is a set of questions reflecting the actual inquiry. There are two characteristics that distinguish such a set of questions from those used in a survey. First, the protocol questions are set for the investigator and not the respondent. The questions are reminders or prompts to the investigator concerning the information that has to be collected. Second, each question should be accompanied by a list of probable sources of evidence that cover documents, observations and interviewees comments.

It is important to remember (Yin 1994) that a particular protocol is designed for data collection from a single case and is not intended to serve the entire project. Therefore, in multi-case situations, a number of protocols will be required.

A Protocol for Field Procedure

1. Find at least three informants for each case study. This is for purpose of data validation.
2. At least two informants should be senior managers, i.e., individuals who are a member of, or report to, the board of directors or similar superiors.
3. Obtain access to informants through a trusted intermediary.
4. Make initial contact with the organisation at the highest level possible.
5. Find a friendly gatekeeper or guide as soon as possible.
6. Tape record all interviews.
7. Support verbal information with documentary evidence where possible.
8. Attempt to secure multiple interviews per site to reduce traveling time.
9. Interview informants in their offices rather than interview rooms.
10. Engage as many members of the staff as possible, such as secretaries and support people, in general conversation about the organisation.

Figure 3.3: A Protocol for Field Procedures

A guide to what is required for the case study report

The guide to compiling the case study report forces the investigator to think about the audience for which the case study is intended early in the case study process. The investigator should be concerned throughout the study with the design of the final report. An outline of the case study report should be included in the case study protocol. This protocol should also indicate to what extent documentary evidence will be used in the final report. Case studies often produce large amounts of documentation and this may be used to produce an annotated bibliography. The bibliography may be helpful to readers in suggesting what is available for further research. Figure 3.4 shows the case study report guide used in this report.

Case study report guidelines

The following are the primary headings that were established as the key focal points of the case study reports. These were established earlier in the research process so that they could be used by the author as a supplementary aide memoir in conducting unstructured interviews with informants.

1. Introduction and general background of the organisation.
2. The state of IT within the organisation.
3. The reasons for the current IT investment decisions.
4. The implementation of the IT investment decision.

Figure 3.4: Case study report guidelines

Using a well-defined protocol, the case study method complies with the basic tenets of the scientific method as it involves classification, observation of relationships, and descriptions of sequences and consequences.

Quantitative and qualitative research and the case study

It is a misnomer to claim that the case study method of research is by nature qualitative. In fact, case studies can be highly quantitative. Wherever possible, purely descriptive data should be converted into quantitative data and then statistical techniques applied. In addition, it is possible to conduct a survey within a case study situation and to use quantitative techniques in the analysis of data so collected. Furthermore, it is worth noting that qualitative data is today more quantitative tomorrow. Quantitative and qualitative techniques are not conflicting but are rather complementary. There will, however, always be qualitative data that cannot be quantified. Although some situations may appear to be similar, they are in fact unique. Statistical comparisons and correlations may actually lead to false assumptions and possibly even to wrong conclusions.

With regard to quantitative and qualitative research, it is important to remember that even in the physical sciences there are several disciplines (such as geology, botany and zoology) that are primarily non-quantitative.

Grounded theory

As the established literature (Chapter 2) did not provide any grand theory, the author employed a method of induction referred to as grounded to establish a theoretical framework within which to conduct the research. Glaser & Strauss (1967) define grounded theory as:

An inductive, theory discovering methodology that allows the researcher to develop a theoretical account of the general features of a topic while simultaneously grounding the account in empirical observations or data.

When applying grounded theory, it is essential that the researcher approaches the inquiry with a reasonably open mind as to the kind of general theory that will emerge from the research (Stake,1994). Of course, preconceptions cannot be entirely avoided, but where possible, they should be minimised. Interviews used to collect data were supported by a schedule to remind the interviewer of the topics being researched.

The aim of the researcher is to obtain an accurate description of the phenomena under investigation. Once this is achieved, the researcher may begin to hypothesize about the nature of the relationships between the observed variables. The grounded theory emerges through the process of concept discovery whereby the researcher moves from data to abstract concepts and categories. This is achieved by the processes of description, definition and specification of relationships. The result could be that the researcher moves to a level of representation where the concepts from a theoretical framework (Huberman & Miles, 1994). It is important to note that, in research, concepts are simply more or less useful and not more or less true and valid (Cohen & Nagel, 1984).

Philosophical stances

DeSanctis (1993) argues that frameworks are useful systems to study but that they do not provide insight into causality or other underlying phenomena. He notes that

... Theoretical thinking on the relationship between Information Technology (IT) investment and organisational effectiveness could lead to fresh streams of empirical work.

The empirical investigation conducted by this book adopted an eclectic approach combining some of the elements of positivism and some of the elements of interpretivism. Rosenthal & Rosnow (1991) defines positivism as the philosophical view that only by supporting explanations with positive facts is it possible to attain an acceptance of objective understanding. Questions and/or hypotheses are stated during the positivist stance and subjected to empirical tests to verify them. Second, an interpretist viewpoint was then adopted with the evidence supplied by the focus group and the opinions of the IT executives (Huberman & Miles, 1994).

SUMMARY AND CONCLUSIONS

In conducting this book's research, a considerable amount of time and attention was devoted to the issue of methodology because the author sees this as the foundation on which the credibility of the research stands. Furthermore, the author believes that as many different approaches to the research problem should be applied as possible. This belief is reinforced by the lack of universally accepted methodologies in research into information systems.

Some of the methods that are used in this research rely on qualitative information, while others are based on highly quantitative approaches. The case study method was primarily used because it allowed IT investment to be examined in a holistic manner within a real life situation. Furthermore, the case study research strategy accommodates the belief in multiple methods of data gathering and data analysis. The focus group was used to obtain access to a number of experts and thus, to widen the range of views collected. It was generally believed that the more informants the better. The focus group also provided an additional step towards triangulation. Finally, the presentation of the results to a number of leading consultants and practitioners was performed to obtain further cross validation of the results.

ENDNOTES

[1]Academics have been interested in this field since the 1970s. However, practitioners and consultants have taken an intense interest in this subject since the end of the 1980s. It is sometimes thought that this business interest was the result of general management being computer literate during the 1980s and as a result more inclined to demand explanations about the effectiveness of their organisations' information technology investments.

REFERENCES

Baran P.A., & Sweezy P.M. (1970). *Monopoly Capital: An essay on the American Order,* Penguin Books, Harmondsworth England.

Barua A., Kriebel C.H. & Mukhopadhyay T. (1991). "An Economic Analysis of Strategic Information Technology investments," *MIS Quarterly*, September.

Bell J. (1987). *Doing your Research Project: A guideline for first-time researchers in education and social science*, Open University Press, Milton Keyness.

Butler-Cox Foundation (1990) "Getting value from Information Technology", *Research Report* 75, June, London.

Chadwick B.A., Bahr H.M. & Albrecht S.L. (1984). *Social Science Research Methods,* Prentice-Hall, Inc. Englewood Cliffs, New Jersey.

Cohen M.R. & Nagel E. (1984). *An introduction to logic and Scientific Method*, Harcourt, Brace and World Inc.

Collins H. (1994).A broadcast video on Science matters entitled "Does Science matter," Open University, BBC, UK.

Daniels J.L. & Daniels N.C. (1993). *Global vision: Building new models for the corporation of the future*, McGraw-Hill New York.

Daniels N.C. (1994). *Information Technology: The management challenge,* Addison-Wesley.

DeSanctis G. (1993). "Theory and Research: Goals, Priorities, and Approaches", *MIS Quarterly*, March, i - iii.

Earl M.J. (1992) "Putting IT in its place: a polemic for the nineties", *Journal of Information Technology*, No 7, 100-108.

Easterby-Smith M., Thorpe R. & Lowe A. (1993). *Management Research: An Introduction*, Sage Publications, London

Edge A.G., & Coleman D.R. (1986). *The guide to Case Analysis and Reporting,* System Logistics.

Einstein A. (1922). *The meaning of Relativity*, Chapman and Hall, London.

Einstein A. (1950). *The Fundamentals of Theoretical Physics in Out of my Later Years* (Philosophical Library).

Farbey B., Land F. & Targett D (1992). "Evaluating investments in IT", *Journal of Information Technology,* No. 7, 109 - 122.

Farbey B., Land F. & Targett D. (1993). *How to assess your IT investments: A study of methods and practice*; Butterworth Heinemann, London.

Galliers R.D. (1991). *Choosing Information Systems Research approaches in Information Systems research*, Alfred Waller.

Glaser B.G. & Strauss A.L. (1967). *The discovery of grounded theory,* Aldine Inc.

Gould S.J. (1980). *The Panda's thumb*, W W Norton & Co.

Haug P. (1996). "Evaluation of Government Reforms, " *Evaluation,* 2(4), October , 417- 430.

Hubbard R. (1979). "Have only men evolved?" in *Women look at Biology looking at Women,* (ed. By Ruth Hubbard, Mary Sue Henifin and Barbara Fried).

Huberman A.M. & Miles M.B.(1994) in *Handbook of Qualitative Research,* edited by Denzin N.K. & Lincoln Y.S, Sage London.

Lee A.S. (1989). "A Scientific Methodology for MIS Case studies", MIS Quarterly, March.

Lubbe S.I. 1994: The impact of Information Technology (IT) on the financial performance of organisations in a developing country, M.Com.-Thesis, UCT, Cape Town.

Nachmias C. & Nachmias D. (1989). *Research methods in the Social Sciences,* Edward Arnold, London.

Remenyi D. (1990). *Strategic Information Systems, current practices and guidelines,* PhD dissertation, Henley - The Management College, Henley-on-Thames.

Remenyi D. (1996). "So you want to be an academic researcher in business and management studies! Where do you start and what are the key philosophical issues to think about?" *South African Journal of Business Management,* 27(1/2), 22 - 33.

Remenyi D. & Williams B. (1995). Some aspects of methodology for research in information systems, *Journal of Information Systems*, No 10, 191-201

Remenyi D., Sherwood-Smith M. & White T. (1996). Information systems management: The need for a post-modern approach, Unpublished report.

Rosenthal R. & Rosnow R.L. (1991). *Essentials of Behavioural Research: Methods and Data analysis,* Second Edition, McGraw-Hill.

Smith N.C. (1990). The Case Study: A useful research method for Information Management, *Journal of Information Management,* 5, 123 - 133.

Stake R.E. (1994) in *Handbook of Qualitative Research,* edited by Denzin N.K. & Lincoln Y.S. Sage London.

Sayer A. (1993). Method in Social research, 2nd Edition, Routledge London.

Trevelyan G.M. (1942). British historian, English Social History, Introduction in The Columbia Dictionary, Columbia University Press.

Yin R.K. (1994). *Case Study Research: Design and Methods*, Second Edition, Sage Publications London.

Chapter Four
The Research

Introduction

This chapter describes how the case study research was conducted. It also provides a summarised account of the organisations participating in the case study research, grouped into industries.

Information Systems in Africa in context

Africa and the other developing countries range from countries with populations that could range from a couple of million people to several million people. Relative to the rest of the world, the developing countries are not substantially industrialised. Some countries could be wealthy countries from an industrial and agricultural point of view and computers have been actively in use in business and industry since the early 1960s when both IBM and ICL opened offices in Johannesburg. Other countries are only waking up to the call of the Internet. Today some countries employ computers in every aspect of industry, business and government, as well as having a relatively high percentage of home computers among the middle class. All the major vendors are present and there is considerable interest in hi-tech.

The business and industrial sectors in some of the developing countries are as sophisticated as anywhere in the world in the use of information systems. South Africa leads the world in deep level mining and supports this activity extensively with computer systems. Some of the developing countries also have a substantial financial services sector that has won international recognition for its excellence in information technology. For example, the First National Bank (FNB) of South Africa was named one of the world's top 100 computer users by *ComputerWorld* in May 1995. In July 1996, FNB also won the prestigious Smithsonian Institute prize for the innovative application of biometrics in their information technology.

Choice of research participants

In order to conduct a research project that would add to the body of knowledge concerning IT investment and IT benefit identification, it was decided to empirically explore actual management practice in the formulation and implementation of IT investment. As mentioned in Chapter Three, a case study research strategy was chosen as the preferred approach to this. The author approached 20 organisations and they all agreed to allow executives to be interviewed concerning their work towards the formulation and implementation of IT investment and IT benefit identification policies. The organisations chosen include both small and large operators in their industry, many of them household names. They have a reputation for high quality products and services. It was expected that they would show the way to others not only in the marketplace, but also in terms of their general management IT investment practices and their use of technology. Figure 4.1 shows a list of the industry sectors from which the participant organisations came.

Total no of Cases	Industrial Sector
3	Educational
2	Local Government
2	Financial
1	Mining
3	Transport
1	Property
2	Publishing
2	Retailing
1	Courier Services
2	Construction
1	Electronics

Figure 4.1: Industrial sectors from which the participating organisations came

The question of confidentiality

Before these organisations would talk to the author, it was necessary to agree that nothing revealed in the interviews that linked their names to the statement could be published without the written consent of the organisations. Individuals were prepared to speak freely about their experiences with IT investment and IT benefits identification; however, on a corporate level, the secrecy ethos so prevalent in these countries made it difficult to obtain corporate approval to publish the material. As a result of the difficulty in obtaining written consent, the actual data has been used, but with false names given to the organisations. This was done in order to publish the data without revealing the identity of the informant or the organisation.

Selecting the organisations for the grounded theory study

With the objective of establishing a grounded theory for the formulation and evaluation of IT investment, the author has undertaken a series of 20 case studies. The case study method was employed because it allows the use of a wide range of research techniques, including interviewing, document reviewing, direct observation, as well as the forming of a focus group for data validation. The number of interviews has been determined, but would include at least two interviews with each of the organisations concerned. Four organisations were visited at least four times each. The interviews were structured following a discussion list designed for the author's own use although informants were allowed as much freedom as necessary within this loose structure and lasted approximately 60 minutes. The case study methodology was selected because the author needed to find answers to *why and how* questions. Lee (1989) supports this research methodology and further claims that case studies capture reality in greater detail and allow analysis of more variables than is possible.

In order to obtain introductions to these organisations as case study subjects, as well as to establish current practices in the computer industry, the author contacted consultants. These included Professor A. Louw (lecturing at Vista University, Welkom, Free State in Sociology) and Mr. Hennie Meyer, a partner of Norval and Associates in Kroonstad, Free State.

The selected organisations are spread over a wide base as was stated. Professor A. Louw recommended the first organisation contacted as one that had made considerable progress towards the formulation and selection of IT investments. From this point, the author obtained information about other projects and organisations which have considerable investments in IT. In other words, IT intensive organisations were the target organisations for this investigation. The author attempted to obtain access to organisations regarded as centres of competence or considered as constituting good practice in the area of IT investment.

Gaining access to these organisations was generally not easy. Each organisation had a different gatekeeper (Reid,1987) with different levels of preparedness to discuss their organisation's experiences. However, having been accepted in the organisations, respondents spoke relatively freely and some supplied written confirmation of their views, as well as organisational documents.

Evidence collected

Evidence collected includes items such as interim reports, published reports, and internal reports such as budgets, strategic plans and other documentation (i.e., testing of hardware IT, etc.). Some of the organisations were not prepared to submit any evidence at all. Our own and outsider's impressions of organisations were prepared in order to use them as part of the case study reports.

The Main Participants

It was decided to conduct in depth case study on four organisations, although 16 additional case studies of organisations were also completed. The author believes that four detailed case studies could be considered an appropriate number in terms of the time and limited resources available for Ph.D. research. The four case studies for this research represent quite different enterprises. The names of the organisations concerned are:

- Couriers — The Fast Couriers
- Transport — IPX

- Mining Mining Information Technology Division
- Financial The Serenity Bank

In the end, all the organisations did not wish to have their names mentioned in this research for fear of attempts to gain a competitive advantage by becoming known prematurely to its competitors. Thus all the names (including the 16 other cases) are fictitious names and are disguised in such a way that will not be easily recognised except to members of the organisations themselves. Although the names are fictitious, it does not mean that the evidence is fictitious. In light of the difficulty in obtaining permission to publish the details of the case studies of the four main contributors, the author felt that it would present unnecessary difficulties and delays to obtain written permission from the other organisations.

Analysis of case study evidence

The main approach to the analysis of the evidence obtained from the case studies was to use content analysis, correspondence analysis and the reduction-data display technique described by Huberman & Miles (1994). Because content analysis was used, a positivist approach was followed supported by a realist and interpretative approach to discuss the results and interpret it in order to apply the conclusions. These techniques require the researcher to carefully comb through the extensive evidence collected from the case study interviews and supplied documents in order to find patterns that display general principles applying to these organisations. As a result of detailed work, empirical generalisations and a theory were developed. These were corroborated using correspondence analysis. Content analysis and correspondence analysis are explained in Chapter 5.

Testing the theory

Because only a relatively small number of organisations were visited as part of the case study phase of the research, it was decided to test the theory developed against a focus group in Johannesburg. To this end, the focus group was assembled with IT experts indicating their willingness to participate in the panel. In addition, the findings of the focus group were taken to some of the original case study informants, as well as the consulting people with whom the author had discussions during the research.

No attempt was made to establish a random sample. Rather, it was believed that the individual organisations, people and consultants used constituted a population in which there was a high degree of awareness and knowledge of IT investments. This approach is justified on the grounds that the author was attempting to establish what constitutes good as opposed to average practice in the field.

Work conducted in collecting the case study evidence

In conducting the four in depth case studies the author visited each organisation at least four times. These visits were to collect evidence by means of structured and semi-structured interviews or discussions. The author met with an average of two informants from each organisation. Several informants were interviewed on multiple occasions. Different informants were deliberately sought in order to obtain a degree of triangulation that assists in the corroboration of the facts supplied. The average length of the interviews were 40 to 60 minutes long. Figure 4.2 shows the number of interviews conducted in each organisation. Virtually all of the informants were employed in the organisations' information systems department or were responsible for the IS.

The entry point or gatekeeper into each organisation differed substantially, and ranged from middle management to senior executives. In addition to the case study participants, the author visited two consultants in order to establish their views concerning the general practice of IS investment in the industry.

The interview schedule

The interviews or discussions were given only a minimal amount of direction by the author. The reason for the decreased direction was to allow informants to select for themselves the issues that they thought were important to the successful formulation and implementation of IT investments and IT benefits identifications. Nonetheless, in order to be able to control the direction of the interview if it strayed off the subject, the author had prepared an interview schedule. The questions used were based on some of the ideas reviewed in Chapter 2 and the M.Com. thesis by Lubbe (1994).

Number of Organisational Cases	Industrial Sector	Title of person Interviewed	No of Interviews
3	Educational	Owner (2) or IT Director	6
2	Local Government	IT manager or Deputy City Treasurer	4
2	Financial	IT managers	6
1	Mining	IT manager	4
3	Transport	IT Consultant or IT managers	8
1	Property	Accountant	2
2	Publishing	IT consultant or IT manager	4
2	Retailing	IT Director or Managing Director	4
1	Courier Services	IT Director	4
2	Construction	Accountant or IT manager	4
1	Electronics	Managing Director	2
	Sub-Total		48
		Interviews with consultants	9
	Total		57

Figure 4. 2: The number of interviews with participating organisations

Since most of the interviews did not stray off the point under discussion, the author only occasionally consulted the interview schedule. The questions in the interview schedule were:

- How does the organisation categorise information technology?

- Of what architecture does the hardware consist?

- Does top management agree with the definition and compilation of the IT in the organisation?

- Has the IT investment decision been tied to any other investment decisions?

- Have IT investment projects been carefully planned and have these investment projects been documented in specific detail including cost-benefit or other types of financial analysis?

- Have these investment projects been thoroughly discussed with potential users before doing the investment?

- Is there a policy decision to centralise/decentralise IT in the organisation (including control of the IT)?

- Have IT investments been coordinated with other interfacing functions?

- Have operators and managers received appropriated training?

- Does the IT Department have greater freedom to respond to exceptions when they occur while doing the IT investment?

- How do they determine whether IT investment has an effect on organisational performance?

A synopsis of the case studies

Details of the case studies grouped into their relevant industries are supplied in Appendix A. Thus only a very brief synopsis of the situations is reported in this chapter.

Case 1: Education industry

The Vision Training College (VTC) has seven distributed sites with their Head Office in Pretoria. VTC was founded in 1982 and has five divisions. IT is used exclusively for their student records and financial systems. VTC indicated that there is no strategic plan at present in place and that it is difficult to invest in IT without getting any directive from top management. IT has not been coordinated with other interfacing functions nor has it had the impact that VTC hoped for. VTC does not have the financial resources to issue all staff with personal computers and that extensive business modeling should be performed to evaluate all alternatives before they invest in IT.

The main reason for placing an IT investment is because VTC considers a general upgrade of IT or the appointment of new staff. The Director of Finance has the authority to approve all IT investments while hidden costs are not included as part of the IT investment. Risks such as theft and damage to IT are experienced, but neither these or other business risks are included as part of the financial calculations of IT investment. Most of their IT investments are gut-feeling investments, while VTC states that they do not measure benefits gained from IT investment. VTC also notes that the effect of culture affects possible benefits they could have received. VTC does not apply post-implementation evaluation of IT investments.

The second organisation, Computer Training (CT), was founded in 1995. The IT cost of CT has been fluctuating a lot because they were not sure how many IT investments they need. All their people using IT have received training to use the IT and the information it generates. The accountant takes all decisions to invest in IT, while the manager prepares these motivations. CT does not consider the portfolio approach to IT investment, because it will not affect the IT investment they place.

An IT investment will only be considered if they need more computer time on which they could generate money. CT measures benefits in financial terms but does not consider hidden costs. CT does not perform post-implementation evaluations while their IT investment evaluation system allows enough freedom to invest in IT.

The last case study, conducted in the educational industry, Computer Training Bureau (CTB), is a franchise-training organisation that used IT to help set their corporate strategy. They were not prepared to link IT to any other investment strategy. CTB is scared that they will become too technically oriented because of the emphasis on computerisation. All the people using computers in CTB have been trained to use them and the information they are generating.

CTB does not take notice of the existence of hidden costs and they are not prepared to include it as part of their IT investment calculations. The manager takes all decisions to buy assets after he and two staff members prepared all the motivations for IT and other assets. Their policy is that all the people working in the organisation should be involved with the IT budgeting. CTB has a problem of combining culture and IT while they note that IT expenses are running away in their business.

Case 2: Local government

The Transitional Local Council (TLC) is a municipality. They are trying to find out if there are any drivers that will help them finalise their IT strategy because they do not have a clearly defined IT strategy at present. The City Treasurer controls all IT while the motivation for IT investments are prepared by each Head of Department and evaluated by the IT department. The City Council approves the final IT budget for TLC. No hidden costs are included in this budget. IT is tested before they buy it while TLC measures the decreases in the number of complaints as part of the benefits they receive. They do not do any post-implementation evaluation of IT investments.

The second case as part of the Local Government industry is the Local Services Council (LSC), founded in 1948. LSC is suffering from a lack of financial resources because of a water and electricity boycott started by the townships. IT is used extensively within the LSC although IT resides as part of the management services division. The City Treasurer is happy with the communication between the different departments and IT. LSC has to work with a fixed IT budget while IT investments have to be motivated twice.

They measure the impact on LSC by noting the decreasing number of complaints. They would like to know how to evaluate the IT investments in more detail, but do not know how to do this. They perform post-implementation evaluation of their IT investments. LSC indicated that it is important to measure the productivity of people using the computer and that they need to teach people to take responsibility for IT investments allocated to them.

Case 3: Financial industry

A consortium of consumers founded the Buy Aid Society (BAS). BAS is a credit card that can be used to purchase a diverse number of goods while BAS receives a collection fee for the services it provides. BAS is concerned with remaining a leader in the field by applying latest technology, although BAS will not usually attempt to be a leading-edge practitioner. BAS used a computer bureau before they started their own IT department in 1989 with the purchase of a mini-computer system. This system was thoroughly tested until they were satisfied with its performance.

The system's purchase was justified because it delivers strategic benefits and although specific and material, these benefits are hard to quantify. The main idea of these benefits is that BAS will be able to sustain the high level of quality service they built their business on, despite new developments in the credit card business. The evaluation of all IS investments is done by the IT manager; e.g., a ratio is calculated of the percentage change in turnover. They are working with a fixed IT budget and do not take any hidden costs into account. They do not perform any post-implementation evaluation of IT investments.

The Serenity Bank was formed in 1838 as an independent asset management, private banking and merchant banking group. During the last two decades Serenity Bank has expanded its activities from those of a pure trust company to include private and merchant banking as well as a range of services, catering to the growing investment needs of both corporate and private clients.

At the beginning of 1995, IS was in control of the information and applications; however, there has been an accelerated move towards employees controlling their information and applications. The IS mission of Serenity Bank today is adding business value. Their IS structure has moved to a system whereby they provide support through help desks and development centres. Serenity Bank cannot perform without IT and that is why all IT investments have been carefully screened and evaluated. All IT investments are measured in terms of productivity and all investments are monitored because benefits are identified before the time. Serenity Bank applies the portfolio approach to IT investments and include hidden costs as part of their IT investments.

Case 4: Mining industry

The Management Information Technology Division (MITD) was founded in 1967. The productivity tools supplied by this IT division are of strategic importance to the gold mines. The division directly affects the working methods of the gold mines in such a way as to produce productivity enhancements, as well as direct improvements in the effectiveness with which gold mines produce their gold. MITD noted that there is a link between the IT and the business strategy.

MITD claims that they handle IT investments differently from the way other organisations handle IT because they do capacity planning on a daily basis and can make instant decisions to expand. MITD recovers their IT costs in total by comparing the history of usage by their clients, monitoring their clients actual usage and calculating a monthly charge back rate. They recover undercharges or pay back over-charges to their clients. IT is purchased after they have tested the item, identified benefits and consulted their members. The post-implementation measurement of IT benefits take place to determine if they are receiving all the benefits they identified during the testing phase[1].

They take hidden[2] costs into account while they ignore intangible benefits[3]. MITD noted that IT can become an inhibitor to change, but would still like to know how to capitalise quickly on unexpected new opportunities. They also would like to investigate the improvement of economies of scale.

Case 5: Transport industry

After many years of state monopoly[4] the transport industry in most of Africa is competitive and to be part of this industry means that all information and control should be tight. Fast Transport (FT) is, however, not a leader in the transport industry and has a lot to learn. IT is not used as intensively as they would like. Their current strategy is defined by their attempts to cope with the main drivers who propel the transport industry. These drivers have been particularly strong during the last couple of years since the government has allowed other people to enter the transport industry. FTs decisions will not affect the competition, but they need to keep track of the decisions their competitors make.

In addition to head count, expenses and assets, there is another resource available to FTs which relates to the support that a particular function can expect to receive from IT investment in order to help the organisation achieve its objective. In this context, IT is being used to directly support the corporate strategy. They measure the increase on turnover if they want to calculate the influence of IT on the organisation as a ratio expressed as a percentage. They do not include hidden costs and include risk as part of the calculations for IT investments. FT does not perform any post-implementation evaluation for their IT investments.

The second organisation, IPX, was founded in 1974. Their business processes are to provide information and IT to all the branches of the IT department. IPX is preparing for the future and would like to keep an eye on the market to ensure that they increase their market share with the help of IT. IPX is therefore setting up bulletin boards to keep in touch with their customers and allow them to communicate with all parties. IT also helps them to make decisions quicker, and they can compute more solutions, helping the managers to consider possibilities and select the answer for their business.

IPX visually monitors the impact on computers on a regular basis. Benefits are only identified at the end of the month when they calculate the percentage change on turnover. They ensure that they receive financial benefits from service level to operational level agreements. IPX include hidden costs identified by using a management program on the computers. IPX uses a gut feeling to perform post-implementation evaluation and would supplement this with end-user interviews.

The third organisation in the transport industry is InterSA. InterSA is a carrier of passengers with its own fleet of buses, competing with the taxis[5]. InterSA searches continually for improvements through innovation and the use of technology and strives constantly to achieve quality. InterSA's strategy is therefore one of differentiation, and it uses IT wherever possible to realise this strategy and to achieve these objectives. The strategy of InterSA forces the IT department to supply information fast and accurately. Although the information is of a historic nature, it will still help the directors. InterSA uses the salary savings as a way of converting benefits into a monetary format.

Case 6: Property

The House and Travel (Trust) organisation was founded in 1952 and their activities incorporate property development, rental, selling real estate and travelling. The four directors take all decisions to buy assets while the accountant prepares motivations for the acquisition of IT. The Trust's IT strategy and their business strategy is linked. IT has also fulfilled promises made and parameters have been set for IT classification. According to the informant, IT affects the productivity of this organisation to a large extent. Productivity is measured in such a way that they could express it in salary savings. The number of complaints play a role to help with the acceptance of IT. Benefits are written down and presented as a motivation to the directors to help them make the final decision. The Trusts perform post-implementation evaluations while threshold investments are handled as any normal IT investment.

Case 7: Publishing

Modern Newspapers publishes a wide range of weekly and monthly publications. Although they do not articulate a corporate strategy, it is clear from observation that it pursues a niche strategy of being a cost leader. They have been using IT since the inception of modern newspapers, but do not have a specific IT department. As was to be expected, IT had been applied extensively to the production area in the newspaper organisation, ranging from receipt of news to typesetting, page composition and layout. However, the organisation did not view applications as providing a competitive edge, so much as ensuring that the company did not fall behind the technology and the economic structure of the industry.

Their independent IT consultant suggested that the main competitive edge application was their marketing system used by a sales team who sold advertising space to clients. This system was not formulated as a strategic system but developed over a period of time as there was no specific implementation plan but rather a series of step-by-step upgrades. The IT consultant prepares all IT investment motivations while the Editor approves them. They do not perform post-implementation evaluations.

The second organisation in the publishing industry is The Nation's Paper, a medium sized organisation publishing a wide range of daily and weekly publications. Their IT applications range from typesetting, page composition and layout. These applications have been well-received by the staff who, after appropriate training, had achieved clear improvements in productivity. However, The Nation's Paper did not foresee such applications as providing a competitive advantage, so much as ensuring that the newspaper fall behind the technology, and losing their competitive edge in the industry. Communication between the different departments is not good. IT improves their productivity as measured in terms of productivity. The IT manager prepares all motivations while the Editor approves them.

Case 8: Retailing industry

Knockers is a retailing organisation. Their computer system is of strategic importance to the organisation for several reasons. The system directly affects the working methods of the organisation in such a way to as to produce substantial productivity enhancements, as well as direct improvements in the effectiveness with which the organisation can control their stock.

All the directors have a good working knowledge of IT, and there is a positive attitude toward its use in the organisation. The directors approve all IT investments and benefits are measured in the form of productivity. They conduct post-implementation evaluations as productivity enhancements in their organisation.

The second retail organisation, Builders, is a large chain of hardware stores in a competitive market with opportunity for the organisation to differentiate its products. They have a standard strategy of cost leadership, and to this end, have used IT very successfully. Builders is highly computerised both from a stock control point of view as well as with more traditional data processing applications[6].

The managing director controls IT and evaluates and motivates all IT investments. The IT department is driven by a cost containment culture[7]. This is reflected in a structured financial approach to system approval and they are trying to become the leaders in their field. Activities to beat the competition is the primary driver that forces Builders to improve their strategic information systems.

Case 9: Courier Services

The Fast Courier's IT department is in the process of a major reorganisation to ensure that their business divisions will improve their performance by focusing directly on profitability and accountability. The IT director prepares all IT motivations and does the presentations to the executive board. However, all benefits of specific IT investments have been identified beforehand because they extended the functionality of the current system and convince management of the value of IT.

Because of future strategic plans, Fast Courier's strategy is tied to the present IT policy, which is that all these investments should be set out in detail explaining all benefits and advantages of the IT investment. They are not doing any post-implementation evaluations, as they are still changing the IT department.

Case 10: Construction

The Construction Company has little opportunity to differentiate their products. Their strategy is therefore of cost leadership and to this end they have used IT successfully. The organisation is highly computerised both from a construction point of view, as well as with more traditional data processing applications. They have, however, appointed a computer shop as a consultant and as a result have the experience that their IT budget is overspent. They do not have an IT strategy in place and lack a financial approach to systems approval. The only post-implementation evaluation they are doing is to inquire about the functionality of the IT.

The second organisation in the construction industry investigated is Corrugated Corporation, one of the largest organisations of construction and plant hire in the Free State. It operates with a strategy of differentiation offering a fast response to its clients, in common with most of the players in its industry. There have been some factors that have helped them to move towards computerisation and specifically towards SIS. The first is the turbulence experienced with the change of the Government in SA and the second is the awarding of contracts to mainly black organisations or organisations that practice affirmative action. This has resulted in construction companies looking for much more control as well as greater insights into the type of risks that they are taking. All these drivers necessitate the changing of their IT policy.

They measure IT benefits on a visual basis and do not include any hidden costs. Corrugated Construction envisages that they will devise a new IT implementation plan; this could affect the benefits they are receiving and measuring. These implementations will be in the form of step-by-step upgrades.

Case 11: Electronics Industry

Freddies Instruments is one of the largest manufacturers and reconditioners of electronic measuring instruments. Freddies Instruments traditionally has held themselves aloof, being a market maker and standard setter rather than a market responder. However, the last couple of years has seen changes in the electronics industry with a dramatic shift in the fundamental economics of instrument manufacture and marketing. For more than six years, Freddies Instruments has identified how they could make extensive use of IT to support its business strategy. They relate to how the IT department supports other departments and implement IT in order to gain competitive advantage. Also how Freddies Instruments can develop policies of its own to survive in their industry.

At the present stage, Freddies Instruments does not measure any benefits and are facing risks if their IT investments do not work out. They need to set the policies for any IT investment and how to measure IT benefits.

Why the above organisations were chosen

The Serenity Bank, IPX and Mining Information Technology Division were chosen as case studies because it is believed that the approach to IT in these organisations represent a fresh approach and good practice for others looking for IT investment approaches. Fast Couriers was chosen because the author received information that this organisation was trying to formulate and implement IT investment policies. As previously mentioned the other 16 organisations were large and smaller organisations, all household names, with a reputation for excellence.

No attempt was made to establish a random sample. Rather a theoretical or "snowball" sample was used. This sampling technique does not necessarily lend itself to being able to generalise the results. For this reason, a different approach is used for the focus group discussion of the research.

Ranking the case studies

In Chapter 5, details are provided as to how the 20 case studies were analysed using both content analysis and correspondence analysis. However, prior to this, it is possible to subjectively rank the case studies in terms of those most effective in their efforts to formulate and implement IT investment and IT benefit policies. Only the four detailed case studies are ranked according to evidence in respect of number of staff members and process quality. The purpose of this ranking exercise is simply to give a first impression of the effectiveness of these organisations with respect to their information systems.

It is clear from the evidence that the Serenity Bank was the most effective in this respect. They had a very clear vision of their objectives and strategies and their formulation and implementation procedures were conducted in a relatively systematic manner designed to support the generic strategy of the bank. The mining organisation was second for the same reasons as the bank. The transport organisation was third in that they had an overall focused strategy to their position in the organisation. However, they did not have a clear view of all the issues which required their attention. The couriers trail in fourth place. They have conceptualised much of the framework they will require for the formulation and implementation of a formal IT investment policy, but have just begun to work in this area, and the investment policy they consider strategic are not the result of formulation and implementation policies, but rather simply consequential to their operational efforts.

ENDNOTES

[1] Testing phase in this instance means that computers are run and physically tested in the organisation.

[2] Hidden costs are those that do not normally form part of the IT investment costs, e.g., travelling to visit similar sites, costs of failed experiments, etc.

[3] Intangible benefits can be seen to provide better information, or can improve the decision making capability but it is difficult to measure and it is even harder to directly link the end benefit to an increase in profitability.

[4] From the 1940s to the 1970s, the state-owned SAR & H had the sole rights to transport in SA.

[5] The word *taxi* in Africa is mainly used to describe a minibus transporting mostly black people.

[6] Traditional in this sense means accounting information systems, stock control systems, etc.

[7] Cost containment meaning cost saving.

REFERENCES

Huberman, A.M. & Miles M.B. (1994) in Handbook of Qualitative Research, edited by Denzin N.K. & Lincoln Y.S., Sage London.

Lee A.S. (1989). "A Scientific Methodology for MIS Case studies", *MIS Quarterly*, March.

Lubbe S.I. (1994). The impact of Information Technology (IT) on the financial performance of organisations in a developing country, M.Com.-Thesis, UCT, Cape Town.

Reid G.C. 1987: International Journal of Social Economics, 14(11).

Chapter Five
The Development of the Theory

Introduction

The objective of this chapter is to describe how the case study evidence was analysed and how the theory was developed. In addition, this chapter discusses how correspondence analysis was used to help validate the findings of the content analysis.

Analysing the case study

Having transcribed the tapes of the interviews and analysed the documentation received, the author was in possession of over 180 pages of textual transcript. It was therefore necessary to analyse the data that had been collected in order to see what general principles relating to the assessment of the effectiveness of IT investment. The main processes used for this analysis and synthesis was content analysis.

Content analysis may be defined as the process of determining or establishing a fuller, detailed meaning of a document, manuscript, speech or any type of communication in a way that is both reliable and replicable. A formal definition of content analysis is supplied by Berelson (1952) as:

a research technique for the objective, systematic and quantitative description of the manifest content of communications.

It is a process of investigating the frequency and intensity with which concepts are addressed in the text. It is a simple but laborious process of closely examining the transcript for concepts, particularly those that are repeated several times. It is by nature a subjective process that relies on what Kerlinger (1969) refers to as manifest content categories being set up by the researcher, and the researcher then counting the number of occurrences of these categories. The establishment of the manifest content categories is one of the main areas of possible subjective bias. The initial categories used in this research were main issues of discussion raised by informants a number of times during the research interviews, and as such were the ones to choose.

Although personal bias will never be totally absent, the author believes that there was relatively little personal bias in the choice of the concepts used here.

According to Berelson (1952), content analysis may be used with different units of analysis including words, themes, characters, items, and space time measurements. In this case, the unit used was themes. This is regarded as one of the more difficult units as a theme can be raised or eluded to in several different ways. For example, productivity as a driver was sometimes referred to during the interviews with the words time better spent, sometimes the word acceptance of IT (would affect productivity was discussed), and sometimes the word complaints about the IT (that could affect productivity)[1], etc.

The result of the content analysis was divided into two main sets of issues, IT investment drivers and then IT benefits were identified. Frequency tables showing the number of occasions in the discussion of the main themes that occurred during the case study interviews were drawn up. In this book, only themes which were raised by informants more than ten times were included in the frequency tables.

SUMMARY RESULTS OF THE CONTENT ANALYSIS

In the following figures, a list of the themes raised by the case study informants and their frequency are shown. These frequency tables are based on the analysis as described. The natures of the drivers are different as some of the drivers originate from the top (e.g., organisational strategy) while some originate from the bottom (e.g., interfacing). It should also be mentioned that the informants specifically named each group, and although some of the themes could be included in both groups, it was decided to keep the groups separate as the informants did not mention the topic under two headings and the author did not want bias to influence the research.

	Themes		Total	%	Accum %
1	Organisational strategy	OS	47	22	22
2	Management decisions	MD	46	22	44
3	Interfacing	FB	28	13	57
4	Quality of Service	QS	27	13	70
5	Evaluation of IT	IF	24	11	81
6	Business modelling	MS	20	10	91
7	Budget	EI	19	9	100
	Total scores		**211**		

Figure 5. 1: Content analysis showing relative frequencies and percentages for IT investment drivers[2]

Figure 5.1 shows that in the transcript of the case study interviews, there were 47 major references to the importance of organisational strategy during the assessment of the effectiveness of IT investment and 46 major references to management decisions during the assessment of the effectiveness of IT investment as well as 28 major references to interfacing function, etc.

IT investment driver[3] descriptions could be formulated as:

Organisational strategy: this theme could be described as the impact of organisational strategy on IT investment. Organisational strategy could be viewed as short and longer range plans that include, for example, the development of new shops that are highly computerised. These also include changing the role of the data processing department to one of distributed processing and to align IS more closely too organisational goals. It can also ensure that the organisations still keep their market share by helping to develop key attributes for the organisation. Overall, organisational strategy is one of the more important drivers cited by managers as a reason for IT investment.

Management decisions: the informants viewed this as a decision by any manager to computerise a certain process, even if it is not normally part of the IT or organisational strategy. According to the informants, many IT investment decisions are made informally in this way. This also includes a gut feeling to invest in IT by managers.

Interfacing: According to the informants, software interfacing is an important IT investment driver. It might save the organisation some money if employees won't need training to use the software and hardware since generations and releases of the software and hardware would look and act the same. Because employees could be used to the way certain software or hardware operates, they would use this to influence organisations to invest in IT that looks or act the same. It therefore includes reasons such as investing in the latest technology and system development ensuring at the same time that the organisation has a competitive edge.

Quality of service: The informants noted that the service level of the organisations could be raised with the help of the IT investment. Also, it was stated that the responsibility for the survival of the organisation could be ensured with the help of the IT investment. The author believes that the nature of this driver is different from the nature of, for example, organisational strategy. It therefore deserves to be a theme in its own right.

Evaluation of IT: The evaluation of IT was mentioned as a driver for IT investment because organisations, while evaluating IT, could notice new benefits which they would like to use in their organisation. This driver could originate from the bottom or from management who could identify the benefit and decide that they would like to receive the benefit that was identified. The evaluation of IT was therefore deemed to be an important IT investment driver.

Business modelling: The informants named the process of creating new models that could be used in the organisation for investing in IT. Informants mentioned that their organisations might decide to 'remodel' the business processes, for example, and discover that they might be able to computerise a process and that this could act as a driver for IT investment. Industry drivers are an important section of this because competitors could be using a business model that can be successfully copied by the organisation.

Organisations could also decide to invest in IT because similar organisations in their industry are doing it.

Budget: Budgeting was described by informants as an important driver. Many organisations budget for IT and eventually end up buying the IT although they might not need it or might decide to go into another direction. Some organisations note that these 'buying of IT out of budgeted costs' on impulse could cause runaway costs that could affect budget as an IT investment driver.

	Themes		Total	%	Accum %
1	Productivity	PB	49	24	24
2	New opportunities	NO	43	21	45
3	Change	CB	27	13	58
4	Competitive advantage	CA	26	13	71
5	Contribution to organisation	CO	26	13	84
6	Increased turnover	IC	21	10	94
7	Reduces risk	RR	12	6	100
	Total scores		**204**		

Figure 5.2: Content analysis showing relative frequencies and percentages - IT benefits[4] identified

Figure 5.2 shows that in the transcripts of the case study interviews, there were 49 major references to the importance of productivity of as one of the benefits during the assessment of the effectiveness of IT investments; 43 major references as to new opportunities for the business; and 27 to changes in the business processes, etc. Of course there were numerous other issues discussed during some of the interviews, such as ethnic culture and lack of black IT people to mention only two, but these were not repeated by other informants and are therefore not included in the above list. The author believed that the list of themes to be considered should not be overwhelmingly long. Theories only incorporate a limited number of themes and in this case it was believed that six to ten themes would be capable of being incorporated into a useful theory or thesis.

IT investment benefits description could be formulated as:

Productivity: This benefit was described by informants as an important benefit that could be derived from using IT. Productivity also could increase if end-users accept the IT. Informants' note that employees will spend their time better because of the application they use, work could be more accurate and complaints will be reduced.

New opportunities: This benefit was viewed by the informants as a benefit that could be described as important for the survival for any organisation. It helps to allocate assets and can help contain the size of the IT department in such a way so as to save resources.

Change: IT investment is not an inhibitor of change and the organisation will therefore make progress. The culture of the organisation could also be affected positively by the IT, according to the informants. This is a benefit that an organisation needs to develop to a large extent.

Competitive advantage: This benefit of IT mentioned by organisations might be of a short duration. The organisational structure will also be affected positively and was viewed by the informants as a benefit, without which organisations would not be able to survive. It also could create new opportunities for any organisation, all part of competitive advantage.

Contribution to the organisation: The informants named this as a benefit because they felt that IT contributes to the organisation, although sometimes it might be in the form of intangible benefits. It can also help the organisation to achieve its objectives.

Increased turnover: This item was named by the informants as a specific benefit. Informants felt that IT makes a specific contribution to the turnover. They also felt that this benefit should be named separately, although it could not specifically be nominated how or why IT made a contribution to the turnover.

Reduces risk: Some informants felt that IT could be a buffer against risk and that having IT in the organisation reduces the risk the organisation has to face. Again the informants felt that they would like this theme to be named, as it would mean that this benefit would be highlighted and organisations should keep track of this benefit.

From the histograms in Figure 5.3 and Figure 5.4 it may be seen that some themes were addressed more frequently than others. The IT investment and IT benefits themes were discussed 10 times or more during the data collection activity.

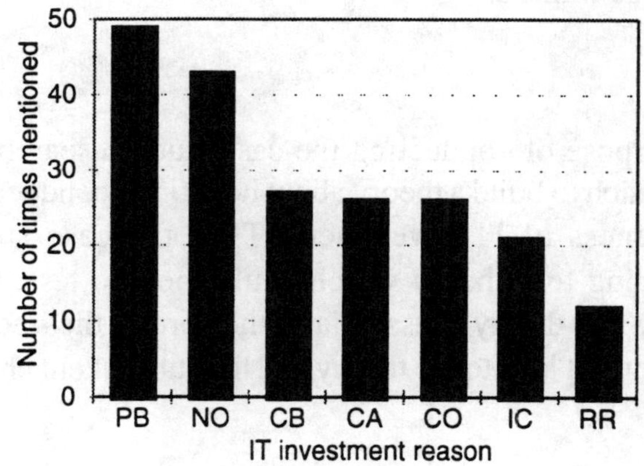

Figure 5.3: Bar chart of the frequency table of the results of the content analysis - IT investment drivers

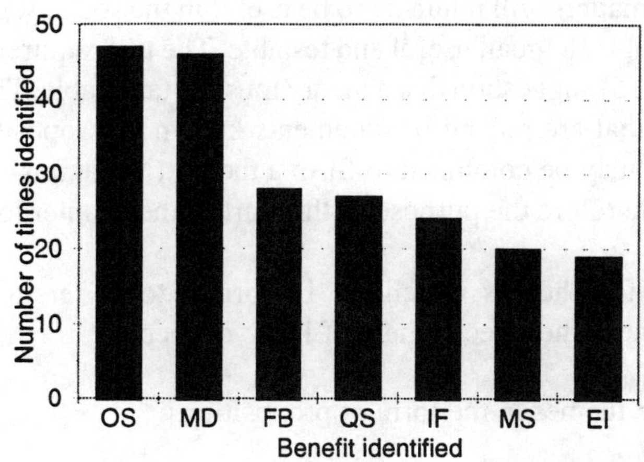

Figure 5.4: Bar Chart of the frequency table of the results of the content analysis - IT benefits identification

It was felt reasonable that a theme must be very important to the informants if it was to be incorporated into the theory that this researched developed. A definition of the importance of a theme to the informants was established pragmatically by asserting that if the theme was mentioned ten times or more it would be included in the theory. Since only seven major IT investment themes and seven major IT benefit themes were identified during the content analysis, it was deemed enough and allowed all the results of the research to be included. This complied with the view that the number of themes in the theory ought to be limited.

The theory

The primary purpose of conducting the case study research was to collect evidence with which to build a theory about how firms conduct the assessment of the effectiveness of IT investment. Thus the case study work was exploratory leading to a theory which could then be tested using a focus group approach. The theory is essentially the core of the book. The work in the earlier chapters all lead to the theory and the subsequent chapters establish its validity.

There are a number of different concepts of theory (Bailey, 1987). For the purposes of this research a theory may be defined as the explanation of a particular phenomenon, or a mechanism which will allow the prediction of how certain matters will interact. To be useful in the social sciences a theory must be sensible, logical, useful and testable. The test requirement relates to Popper's (1975) suggestion that a theory must be falsifiable. Theories consist of concepts that are related in statements known as propositions. A set of propositions may be combined to form a theory (Nachmias and Nachmias, 1989). It is therefore the purpose of this part of the chapter to:

- establish the themes which are important to understand during the assessment of the effectiveness of IT investment.
- state these themes in the form of propositions.
- combine these propositions into a theory.

These issues relate directly to the research questions in Chapter 2 that could be summarised to how organisations handle effective IT investments.

Theory formulation

The purpose of developing the theory is to explain how management goes about the business to assess the effectiveness of IT investments. If a satisfactory explanation can be developed, it could provide a basis for evaluation of IT investment management and allow an understanding as to the likely success of IT investment in a particular firm, according to whether or not management complies with the procedures expressed in the theory.

From the results of the content analysis of drivers for IT investment, it can be deduced that organisational strategy and management decision factors are very important drivers for the placement of an IT investment. From the discussions with the informants, it is apparent that the two drivers are often considered together.

The other IT investment drivers of interfacing, quality of service, evaluation of IT and business modelling are also important and must be incorporated into the theory. IT budgeting is also seen as an important issue. However, in the case of IT investment, it is the absence of emphasis of the necessity to do what is important.

From the results of the content analysis of drivers for IT benefits, it can be deduced that productivity and new opportunities are very important benefits organisations expect to receive from an IT investment. From the discussions with the informants, it is reasonable to assume that the two issues are often considered together.

The other IT benefits of change in the business processes, competitive advantage, contribution to the organisation and increased turnover are also important and must be incorporated into the theory. Risk reducing is also seen as an important issue. However, in the case of the effectiveness of IT investment, it is the absence of the necessity to do this which is important.

In order to assist with the interpretation of the results of the content analysis three diagrammatic conceptual frameworks (Miles & Hubermann: 1984) were developed which indicate how these themes are linked. These are shown in Figures 5.5, 5.6 and 5.7.

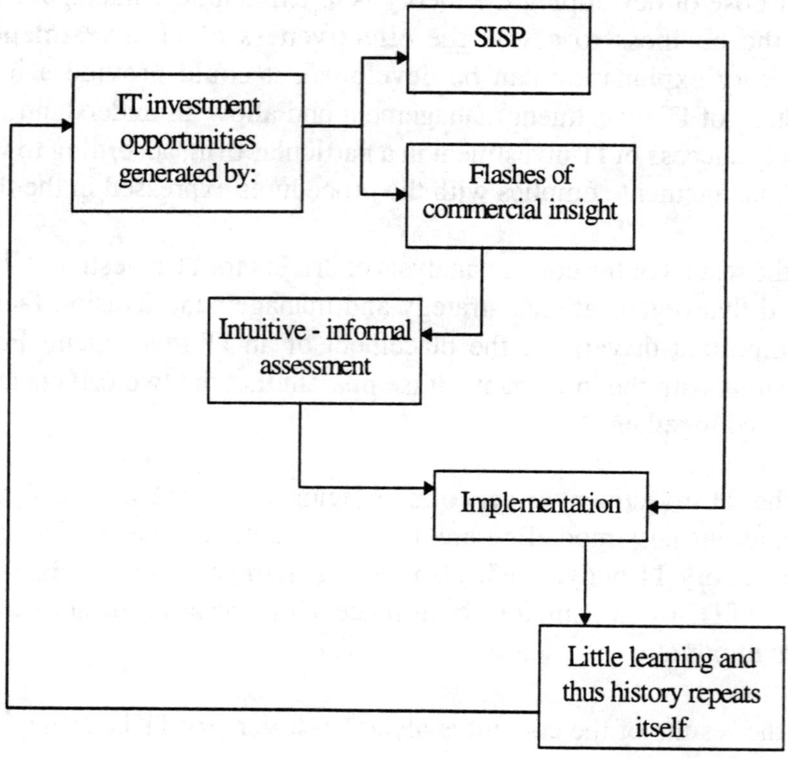

Figure 5.5: A traditional view of IT investment processes in organisations

Figure 5.5 addresses the traditional IT investment issues as they are presently being used by the organisations studied. This diagram shows how IT investment originates. Some IT investments are decided upon during the strategic information systems planning process (SISP) but most of the time as a result of gut-feeling processes ("flashes of commercial insights"). It can be noted that more than 70% of the organisations are not following any formal processes but rather look at opportunities or market orientation.

These investments are therefore assessed during an informal process according to the informants of most of the organisations. After this assessment, the IT investments are placed and implemented. Little learning takes place during the whole IT investment process and history just repeats itself. The processes are thus repeated by most of the organisations (more than 70%) without any learning.

The approach to the assessment of the effectiveness of IT investment planning, as described in Figure 5.5, exhibited not many characteristics, approaches and techniques.

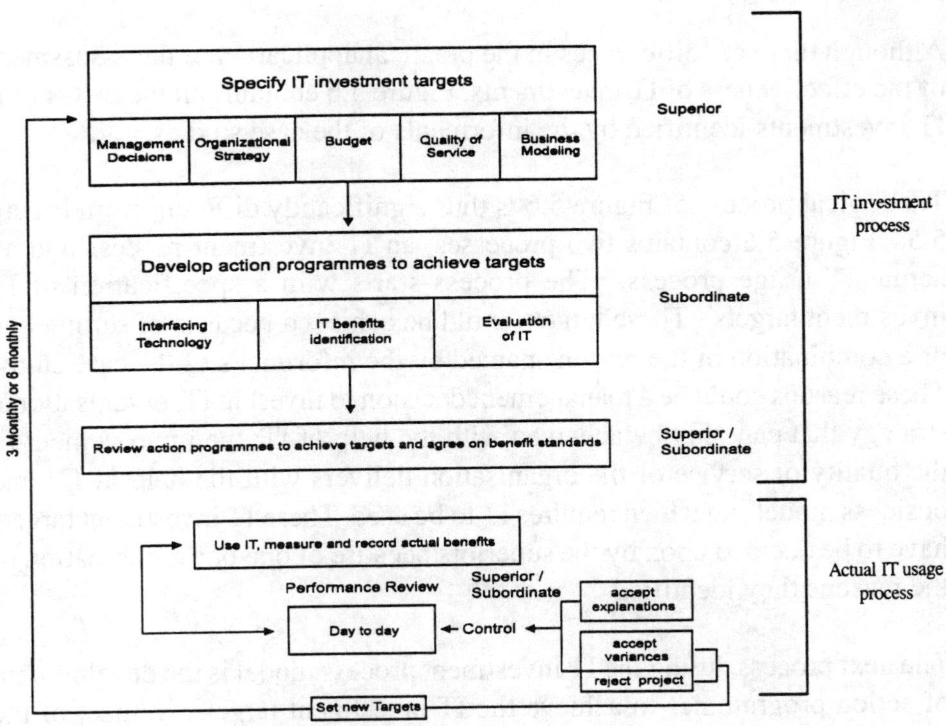

Figure 5.6: The proposed IT investment process and usage model

Figure 5.6 therefore displays a new approach to the assessment of the effectiveness of IT investments. The figure exhibits the specification of IT investment targets and techniques that could be used during the IT investment process. In most of the processes, it differs significantly from Figure 5.5 - the basic principles underlying traditional IT investment processes.

One of the differences could be that a learning process[5] is applied to each IT investment, Figure 5.5 describes an annual process and the flow of information was also not in a programmed way. IT managers could have been in the embarrassing position (because of the uniqueness of the event) of not knowing about IT investments or why they were placed. Every manager feels that he/ she has the responsibility of keeping his superiors informed of the IT investments.

Although there are differences in the practical application of the assessment of the effectiveness of IT investments, Figure 5.6 contains all the drivers for IT investments identified by the informants of the case studies.

The logical process of Figure 5.6 is thus significantly different from Figure 5.5. Figure 5.6 contains two processes, an IT investment process and an actual IT usage process. The process starts with a specification of IT investment targets[6]. These targets could be achieved because of setting one or a combination of the reasons named by the informants of the case study. These reasons could be a management decision to invest in IT; organisational strategy that can only be achieved with the help of IT; the improvement of the quality of service of the organisation delivers with the help of IT; and business modelling which requires IT to be used. These IT investment targets have to be decided upon by the superiors because of one or a combination of the reasons they identified.

The next process during the IT investment process model is the development of action programmes to achieve the IT investment targets. In most of the cases, the subordinate expected to achieve the target develops these action programmes. The superiors could supply an in-depth investigation of the reasons for the further development of the IT investment action programmes. These are: an action programme that can set the software interfacing for IT investments where the superiors decide to use the same approach to allow staff ease of use; an action programme that can help with the identification of benefits by stating the benefits needed to achieve the IT investment targets (Figure 5.7); and to develop an action program that can help with the evaluation of the proposed IT investment. Once these action programmes have been developed, a commitment to achieve the target is made between the superior and the subordinate. This could be done by reviewing action programmes and to agree on a certain level of benefits to be achieved. They will also agree on the actual evaluation approach of the IT investment, thereby ensuring that the IT investment will be the one needed by the organisation.

The IT investment process involves finalising the expected standard of performance in terms of the previously agreed upon action programme before using the IT. The user should then record actual benefits as the IT is being used, compare the actual benefit with the expected standard on a daily basis and any discrepancies should be noted. On a three-monthly or six-monthly basis, a major review of IT investment targets is undertaken, at which stage new targets are set.

IT investment targets (see Footnote 2 and Figure 5.6) will keep on changing because the IT goal posts keep on moving. IT investment objectives may not be reached as a result of these changes. The IT investment action plans should thus include strategies to:

- accept explanations for the differences (variances) between actual IT benefits and the benefit standard agreed upon. No changes are thus made to the IT investment targets and the benefit standards.

- accept variances in the light of changed circumstances but new targets will have to be reviewed and new benefits standards have to be set. The process will thus start all over again.

- possibly make a drastic decision whereby the superior decides to reject the IT investment totally and set new targets, and then specifies a new IT investment action plan, starting the process all over again.

The identification of IT benefits as set out below (Figure 5.7) is a strategy suited to IT investment environments keeping risk (uncertainty) in mind.

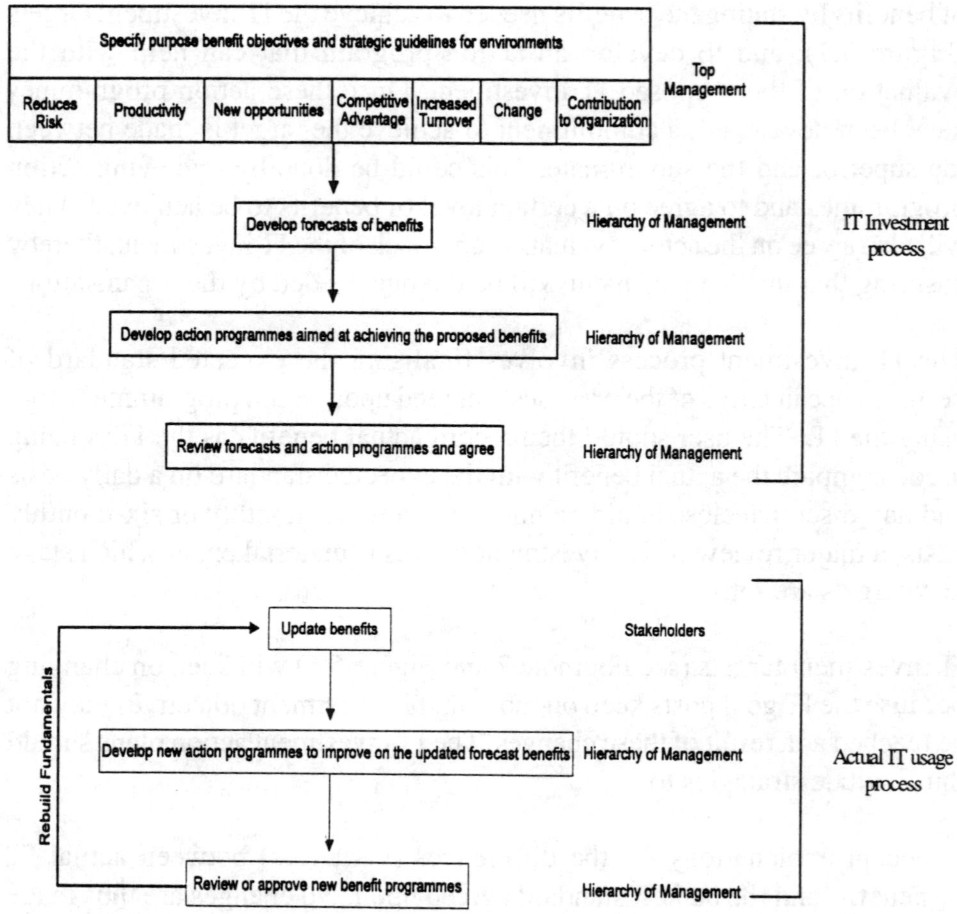

Figure 5.7: A perspective on IT benefits - the IT investment process and the IT usage process.

Figure 5.7 describes the IT benefits identification during the IT investment and the IT usage phases. The process of IT benefit specifications, as summarised by Figure 5.7, seems to be appropriate. During the IT benefits measurement processes, satisfactory performance is equated with the ability of managers to continuously generate action plans aimed at improving the effectiveness of the IT investments and not by their ability to achieve a benefit based on a set of assumptions that can change over time.

Figure 5.7 demonstrates the important process of IT benefits management. Top managers might have to specify benefit purpose objectives and strategic guidelines for the IT investment environment using the IT benefit themes identified by the informants during the case studies. These objectives and strategies could therefore specify one or more of the benefit themes or all of the benefit themes. Based on these benefit themes, the managers could develop forecasts of the benefits expressing at the same time to what extent it could affect the IT investment and the organisation. Action programmes could then be developed to help achieve the benefit by the managers who would review the forecasts and action programmes and agree on accepted levels for the IT benefits to be reached.

The stakeholders will have to rebuild the fundamentals required to achieve the benefits agreed upon by top management. As IT is used, action programmes need continuously to be improved and the forecast level of benefits adjusted. The action would thus require involvement by managers before, during and after the IT investment process.

If this IT investment process, as illustrated in Figure 5.6, is compared with the process of IT benefit realisation as illustrated in Figure 5.7, it becomes clear that the proposed IT investment process is an ideal process aimed at improving the assessment of the effectiveness of IT investments. IT realisation planning is the ideal approach during the control of IT investments and SISP that could be aimed at improving all areas of IT investment.

The management of IT investments would require the following information:

i. Internally generated information dealing with IT benefits as identified by the informants during the case study.

ii. Internally generated external information that has been formally gathered, processed and stored, dealing with the assessment of the effectiveness of IT investments that is critical to the successful management of IT investments.

iii. A variety of specialised information dealing with specific decision situations that defied any attempt at prior definition (intangible benefits).

Empirical Generalisations

Using the above content analysis (Figure 5.1 and 5.2) and the evidence suggested by the various informants the following generalisations have been derived or synthesised:

- IT investments occur as a result of targets identified by top management because of one or more drivers classified in Figures 5.1 and 5.6.

- The organisation's response to the opportunity for the assessment of the effectiveness of IT investments is influenced by the themes affecting the IT investment process. Both tangible and intangible benefits are included. The precise theme directly dictates the evaluation process that will be used. Tangible benefits will be measured financially and intangible benefits will be measured qualitatively.

- The decision to invest resources into IT is taken with the help of action plans (a strategy) aimed at achieving the IT investment targets like efficiency (quality of service), improving business processes (modelling), etc. with attention to detail concerning the ability of managers to review and update these action programmes in conjunction with subordinates (see Figure 5.6).

- Attention is given to specification of benefit objectives (productivity, profitability, etc.), realisation of IT benefits and to communication with staff members at all levels of the hierarchy of the organisation (see Figure 5.7).

These propositions have been expressed in this way because unlike hypotheses that strictly have to be stated in a testable form (which allows the relationship between two or more variables to be examined). Empirical generalisations do not have this format requirement. An empirical generalisation is a proposition which is derived as a result of an exercise in deduction whereby propositions are constructed after observing themes and relationships in a real life, i.e., empirical situation. They do not necessarily have to express in terms of the relationship between two or more variables. In the same way, while hypotheses may be tested empirical generalisations may also be tested to see if they have the significant support or practitioners in industry. These empirical generalisations will be tested using a panel discussion to see if they can be applied in a more general way.

The thesis

The four empirical generalisations may now be combined into a theory which explains how the assessment of the effectiveness of IT investment is formulated and implemented.

IT investments occur as a result of targets identified by top management because of one or more drivers classified in Figure 5.6. These targets are developed into action plans in conjunction with subordinates and these two groups regularly review them.

The organisation's response to the opportunity for the assessment of the effectiveness of IT investment is influenced by the themes affecting the IT investment process as shown in Figure 5.7. The decision to invest resources into IT is taken with the help of action plans (a strategy) aimed at achieving the IT investment targets like efficiency (quality of service), improving business processes (modelling), etc., with attention to detail concerning the ability of management to update the action programmes. Attention is given to the specification of benefit objectives (productivity, profitability, etc.), realisation of IT benefits and to communicate with staff members at all levels of the hierarchy of the organisation. It is important to include all benefits, both tangible and intangible. Evaluation is conducted regularly for control purposes and the result of the evaluation may be one of the three outcome described in Figure 5.6. When the evaluation dictates a change to the system, benefit profiles and programmes are updated and fundamentals are rebuilt as per Figure 5.7.

The above theory and empirical generalisations comply with the requirements of sensible, logical as well as testable or falsifiable.

Since the theory is developed directly from the empirical generalisations, to establish the theory's acceptance all that needs to be done is to test the empirical generalisations. This was done by using a focus group. Chapter 6 considers the results of the focus groups and practitioner presentations.

However, while proceeding with the focus group to test the empirical generalisations, correspondence analysis was used to help corroborate how the findings of the content analysis interpret the theory. As correspondence analysis provides a perceptual map of the data, it can provide a deeper insight into the multivariate nature of the data.

Correspondence analysis

Correspondence analysis was developed in France, being the brainchild of Jean-Paul Benzecri. The English word, correspondence, is derived from the French word *correspondance*, which has a different meaning of system of association (Greenacre, 1984). Thus in English, the term association analysis might in fact be more appropriate.

Correspondence analysis is an exploratory data analysis technique for the graphical display of contingency tables and multivariate categorical data (Green *et al.*,1989). It's objective is to represent data graphically, in such a way that the nature of the associations among the variables will be seen, and that they can be more easily interpreted, according to Greenacre (1984).
Correspondence analysis is a technique for displaying the rows and columns of a data matrix (primarily, a two-way contingency table) as points in dual low-dimensional vector spaces.

It is a mathematical procedure that uses categorical data in the form of two-dimensional rectangular matrix of non-negative numbers as a two-contingency table for the geometric mapping of frequency or binary data. The two-dimensional matrices actually used were the frequency tables in Figure 5.8 and Figure 5.16 showing the occurrence of themes discussed during the case study interviews. The primary result of the correspondence analysis is a map identifying the row and column attributes as points in a space of two or more dimensions. This is a graphical display or perceptual map that represents the relative positions or grouping of the various themes listed in the matrix or frequency table. The perceptual map may be presented in two or more dimensions. However, it is the object of correspondence analysis to present the results in as simple a form as possible.

The main themes underlying correspondence analysis are profile, mass and chi-square distance. Correspondence analysis is similar in style to principal component analysis, but in correspondence analysis, the total variation in the data matrix is measured by the usual chi-squared statistic for the two-column independence, and it is this quantity which is decomposed along the principal axis (Greenacre, 1984).

The use of correspondence analysis

Introduction to correspondence analysis

Content analysis revealed that the case study participants were concerned mainly about seven major themes. The next step in the theory formulation was to establish how these themes related to each other and to the different participating enterprises. Correspondence analysis is an excellent vehicle for so doing.

The use of correspondence analysis to analyse IT investment drivers

Figure 5.8 shows the result of the content analysis detailed by participating industry. The scores of each of the eleven industries in the case study research are shown separately.

			1	**2**	**3**	**4**	**5**	**6**	**7**	**8**	**9**	**10**	**11**	**Total**
1	Organisational strategy	OS	9	1	3	5	8	5	2	3	5	2	4	47
2	Management decisions	MD	8	2	6	4	5	5	2	6	4	2	2	46
3	Interfacing	FB	1	1	5	2	14	0	2	0	0	0	3	28
4	Quality of Service	QS	2	1	3	2	4	10	0	2	0	0	3	27
5	Evaluation of IT	IF	1	0	3	4	3	5	2	1	3	0	2	24
6	Business Modelling	MS	2	1	4	1	4	0	0	5	0	0	3	20
7	Budget	EI	0	0	4	4	4	5	0	0	0	0	2	19
	Total		**23**	**6**	**28**	**22**	**42**	**30**	**8**	**17**	**12**	**4**	**19**	**211**

Figure 5.8: Summary results - IT investment drivers

Note the abbreviations used for the different themes, i.e. OS for organisational strategy, MD for management decisions, QS for quality of Service, etc. used in Figures 5.1 and 5.8. Figure 5.9 is a table defining the different industries by number.

Industrial Sector	**No**
Transport	1
Electronics	2
Educational	3
Local Government	4
Financial services	5
Mining	6
Property	7
Publishing	8
Retailing	9
Courier	10
Construction	11

Figure 5.9: Industries and their number

All sections of Figure 5.8, i.e., rows 1 to 7 for all columns were extracted for processing using a correspondence program. The program used was xlSTAT, developed by Thierry Fahmy of the French Department of Agriculture in Paris. xlSTAT produces seven tabular reports and one graph. The seven tables show the basic data that is used by the system to produce the graph. For the purposes of this research, two of these reports are of the utmost importance. These are the inertia report and the graph. The *INERTIAS (Eigen values) and PERCENTAGES OF INERTIAS* are both a table and a histogram and are shown in Figure 5.10 and Figure 5.11. This figure provides inertia or Eigen values. In this context, inertia is defined as a measure of the total variability in the original data set. This report determines the number of dimensions required to explain the original data set. It may be seen from Figure 5.10 (IT investment drivers) that one dimension will explain 50% of the total data variability and that two dimensions will explain 79% of the variability.

Therefore by using two dimensions, more than three-quarters of the variability may be explained.

No	Inertias (Eigen values)	Percentages
1	0.1371	50
2	0.0788	29
3	0.0299	11
4	0.0198	7
5	0.0082	3
6	0	0

Figure 5.10: Inertia or Eigen values - IT investment drivers

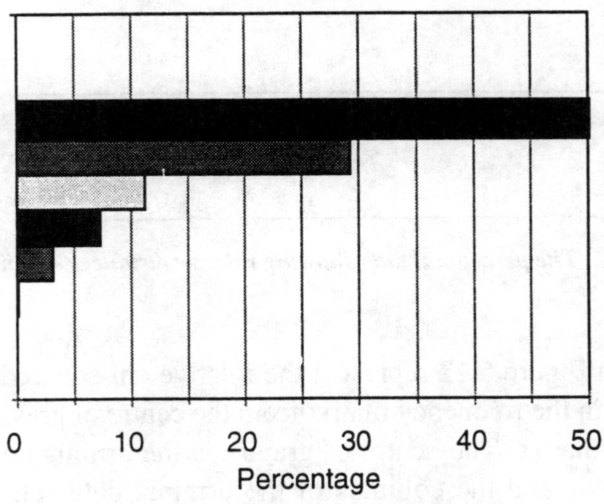

Figure 5.11: Histogram - IT investment drivers

Figure 5.12 is the perceptual map or graphical display that shows the relative position of the different themes and the different participating informants. This is displayed on the next couple of pages. As previously mentioned OS, MD and FB represents respectively organisational strategy, management decisions and interfacing etc. And I1, I2 and I3, etc. represent the different participating industries. The I was used to indicate column data and the 1 - 11 as per Figure 5.8 to represent the different industries.

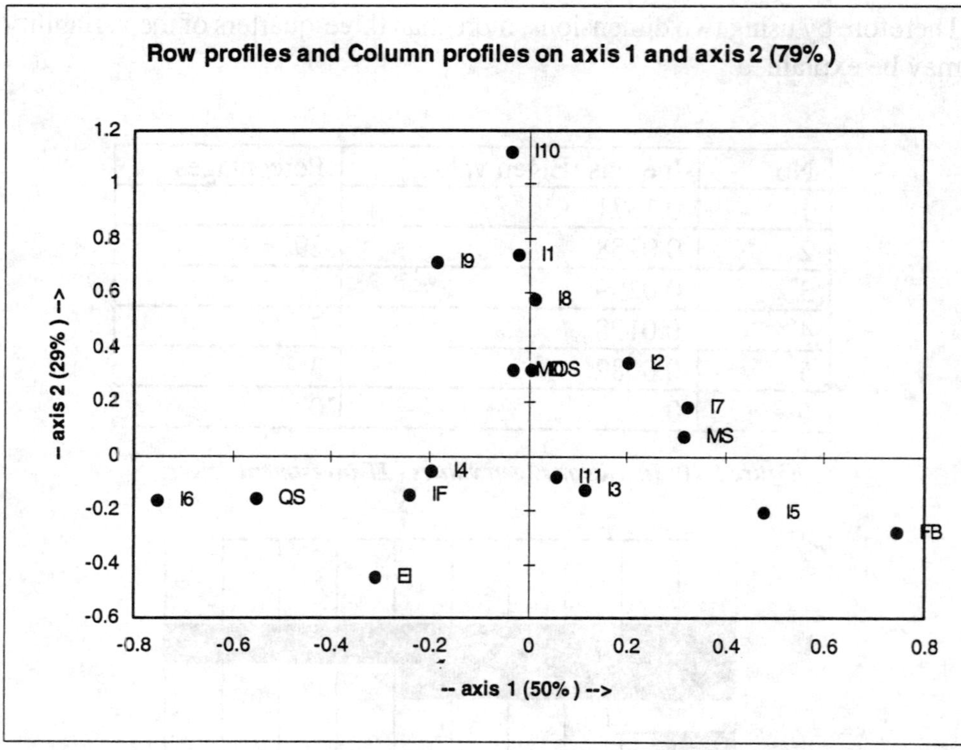

Figure 5.12: The perceptual map showing relative distances - IT investment drivers

The axes in Figure 5.12 represent the relative chi-squared distances of the data points in the frequency matrix from the centre of gravity of the original data set or matrix. The centre of gravity is the arithmetic mean profile of both the rows and the columns of the original data set. The chi-squared distance is a measure of the deviation of the observed distances from the expected distances under some assumed model that is frequently a no association model. The axes are purely numerical scales that are produced to show relative distance from the centroid in a graphical way. These axes may be thought as two artificial variables synthesised from the original data set which give the maximum explanation of the differences and the similarities between the originally observed values. Both row data values and the influence of the column values associated with that row variable determine the position of the row data points. The perceptual map is the key product of correspondence analysis that shows how the row and column variables may be grouped. It is up to the analyst using the correspondence analysis to actually attribute meaning to these axes. Figure 5.13 shows the centre of gravity and the chi-squared distances for the IT investment drivers.

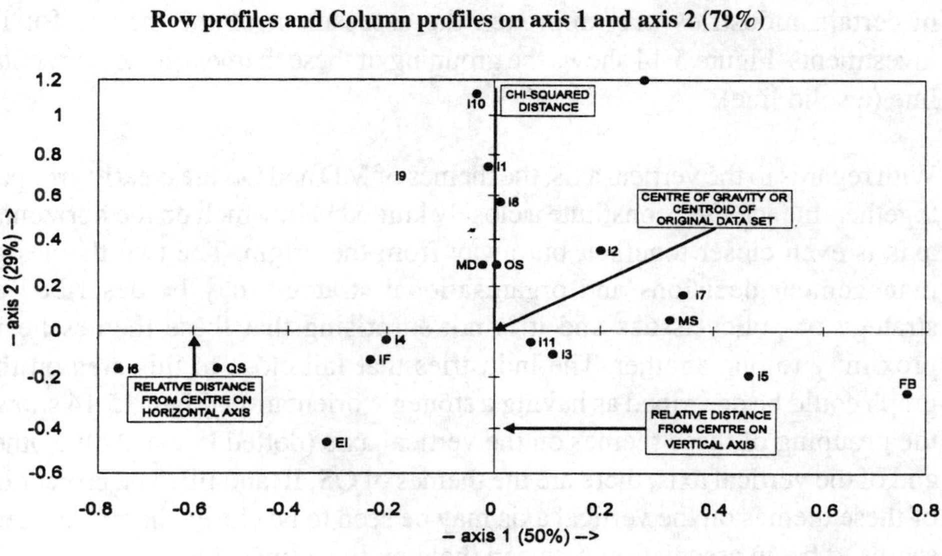

Figure 5.13: The perceptual map with the intercept, axes and distances explained

From Figure 5.12, it is possible to see that some of these themes and participating industries may be conveniently grouped together. For example, the three themes IF, QS and EI are all to the left of the intersection of the axes, and the themes MS and FB are all to the right of the axes. The themes of quality of service, evaluation of IT, and budgeting may all be described as being of an evaluative orientation, and it is not surprising that these themes lie in proximity on the horizontal axis to one another. The industries that fall close to this area on the graph could be described as having an evaluative approach to IT investment[7]. In a similar way, business modelling and interfacing may be described as being part of the business processes and it must be noted that these themes lie in proximity on the horizontal scale to one another. The fact that these themes are also not highly spread on the vertical axis support the grouping done on the horizontal axis. The industries which fall close to this area on the graph could be described as having a business process focus to IT investments. These two variables represent a bi-polar dimension with evaluative orientation on one end of the scale and business processes on the other. Thus two new variables have been defined for the horizontal axis which offer some insight into the way organisations in certain industries may approach the assessment of the drivers for IT investments. Figure 5.14 shows the grouping of these themes on the horizontal line (a solid line).

With regards to the vertical axis, the themes of MD and OS are clearly grouped together. In fact, they constitute a closely knitted pair, which on the horizontal axis is even closer together, but away from the origin. The two themes of management decisions and organisational strategy may be described as strategy or policy issues and it is not surprising that these themes lie in proximity to one another. The industries that fall close to this area on the graph could be described as having a strategic orientation. Figure 5.14 shows the grouping of these themes on the vertical axis (dotted lines). At the other end of the vertical axis, there are the themes of QS, IF and FB. The projection of these themes on the vertical axis may be seen to be close; therefore, there seems to be an association between them on this dimension.

Row profiles and Column profiles on axis 1 and axis 2 (79%)

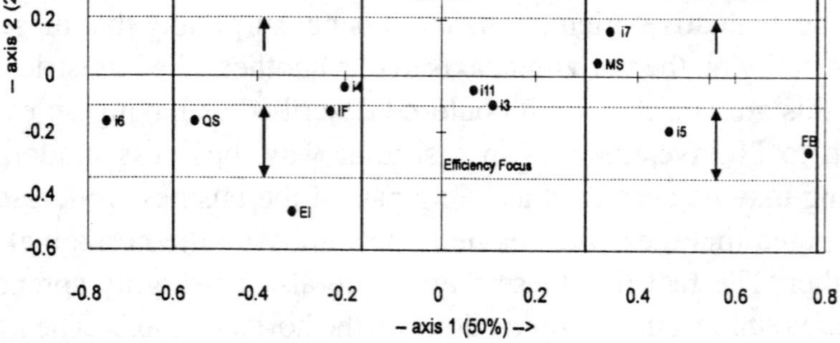

Figure 5.14: The perceptual map with the horizontal and vertical axis defined

All the themes, that is interfacing, evaluation of IT and quality of service are efficiency issues and industries in this area could be described as having their focus on efficiency. Thus provides the second bipolar or vertical axis.

Figure 5.15 shows the full system of grouping of these themes. Themes that are all grouped together on the perceptual map may be thought of as a type of correlation in that the association shows that there exists a relationship between these variables. The perceptual map does not indicate the type of relationship. The specification of the nature of the relationship depends on the environment being described by the correspondence analysis. Therefore, from the correspondence analysis described in this chapter, the author can state that the organisations that participated in the case study as informants perceive the issues of quality of service, evaluation of IT, and interfacing as being associated.

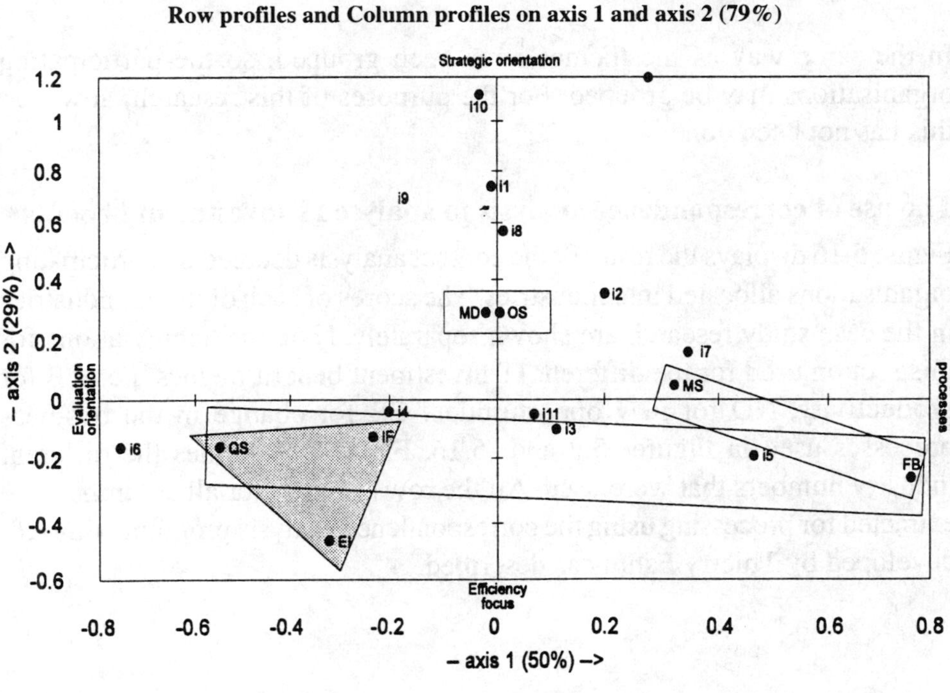

Figure 5.15: The perceptual map showing the horizontal and vertical axes

The issues of management decisions and organisational strategy have all similar values on the horizontal and vertical axis. Therefore, they can be seen as a group or a band of issues. However, two points here are important: Correspondence analysis provides a measure of theme quality, which may be defined as the extent to which variables are well represented in the number of dimensions being presented. The quality rating for business modelling is low and therefore not necessarily close to the horizontal axis, since it is actually on a third dimension which cannot be represented on a piece of paper. The other variables of interfacing have different vertical axis score. This suggests that interfacing are treated entirely differently. This perceptual map shows interfacing being somewhat of an efficiency focus issue, whereas business modelling appears to be more relevant to strategic issues. This does not correspond to the idea that some organisations will use the process of modelling their business processes as a motivation for IT investments and this could be reflected in their strategy.

In the same way as the themes have been grouped, so the participating organisations may be grouped. For the purposes of this research, however, this has not been done.

The use of correspondence analysis to analyse IT investment benefits

Figure 5.16 displays the result of the content analysis detailed by participating organisations allocated into industries. The scores of each of the 11 industries in the case study research are shown separately. Note the abbreviations for this section used for the different IT investment benefit themes, i.e., PB for productivity, NO for new opportunities, CB for change in the business processes used in Figures 5.2 and 5.16. Figure 5.9 defines the different industry numbers that were used. All the rows (1 to 7) for all columns were extracted for processing using the correspondence analysis program (xlSTAT) developed by Thierry Fahmy as described.

			1	2	3	4	5	6	7	8	9	10	11	Total
1	Productivity	PB	2	0	5	6	11	6	4	3	4	0	8	49
2	New Opportunities	NO	3	0	4	5	10	8	2	3	3	2	3	43
3	Change	CB	3	2	6	1	6	5	2	0	0	0	2	27
4	Competitive Advantage	CA	4	0	2	2	6	3	2	2	3	0	2	26
5	Contribution to Organisation	CO	6	1	3	0	4	0	1	2	4	2	3	26
6	Increased Turnover	IC	4	0	2	2	4	5	0	0	2	0	2	21
7	Reduces Risk	RR	1	0	1	2	3	3	2	0	0	0	0	12
	Total		**23**	**3**	**23**	**18**	**44**	**30**	**13**	**10**	**16**	**4**	**20**	**204**

Figure 5.16: Summary results - IT investment benefits

No	**Inertia's (Eigen values)**	**Percentages**
1	0.0974	58
2	0.0407	24
3	0.0226	13
4	0.0063	4
5	0.0008	1
6	0.0001	0

Figure 5.17: Inertia or Eigen values - IT benefits

The reports determine the number of dimensions required to explain the original data set. It may be seen from Figure 5.18 (IT investment benefits) that one dimension will explain 58% of the total data variability, and two dimensions will explain 82% of the variability. Therefore by using two dimensions, more than three-quarters of the variability may be explained.

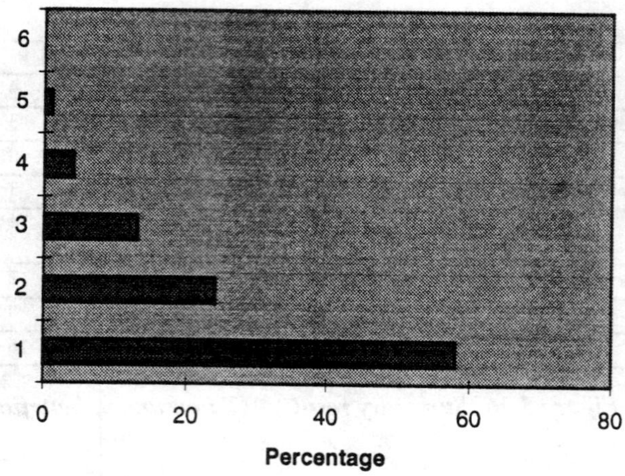

Figure 5.18: Histogram - IT benefits

The next report is the perceptual map or graphical display that shows the relative position of the different themes and the different participating informants. This is displayed in Figure 5.19. As previously mentioned PB, NO, CB, etc. represent respectively productivity, new opportunities, change, etc. and I1 I2, I3, etc. represents the different participating industries. The I was used to indicate column data. Numbers1 to 11, as per Figure 5.19, represent the industries.

As was explained, the axes in Figure 5.20 represent the relative chi-squared distances of the data points in the frequency matrix from the gravity of the original data set or matrix. The centre of gravity is the arithmetic mean profile of both the rows and the columns of the original data set. The chi-squared distance is a measure of the deviation of the observed distances from the expected distances. The axes are purely numerical scales that are produced to show relative distance from the centroid in a graphical way. These axes may be thought of as two artificial variables synthesised from the original data set, which give the maximum explanation of the differences and the similarities between the originally observed values.

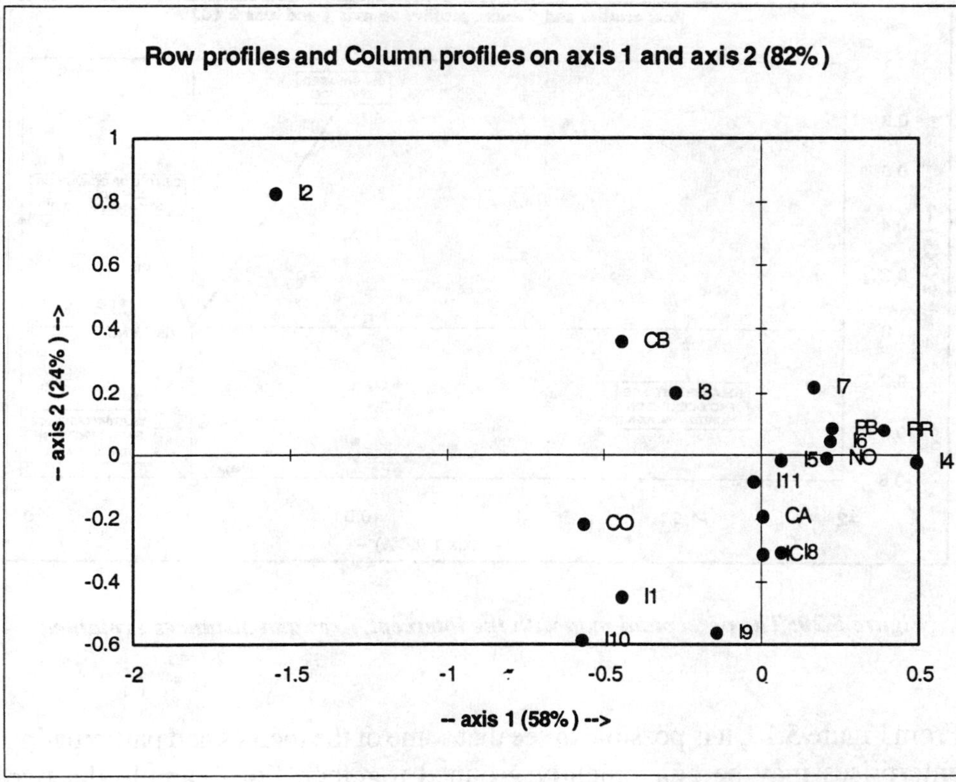

Figure 5.19: The perceptual map showing relative distances - IT investment benefits

Both row data values and the influence of the column values associated with that row variable determine the position of the row data points. The perceptual map is the key product of correspondence analysis that shows how the row and column variables may be grouped. It is up to the analyst using the correspondence analysis to actually attribute meaning to these axes. Figure 5.20 shows the centre of gravity and the chi-squared distances for the IT investment drivers.

It is up to the analyst using the correspondence analysis to actually attribute meaning to these axes. Figure 5.20 shows the centre of gravity and the chi-square distances.

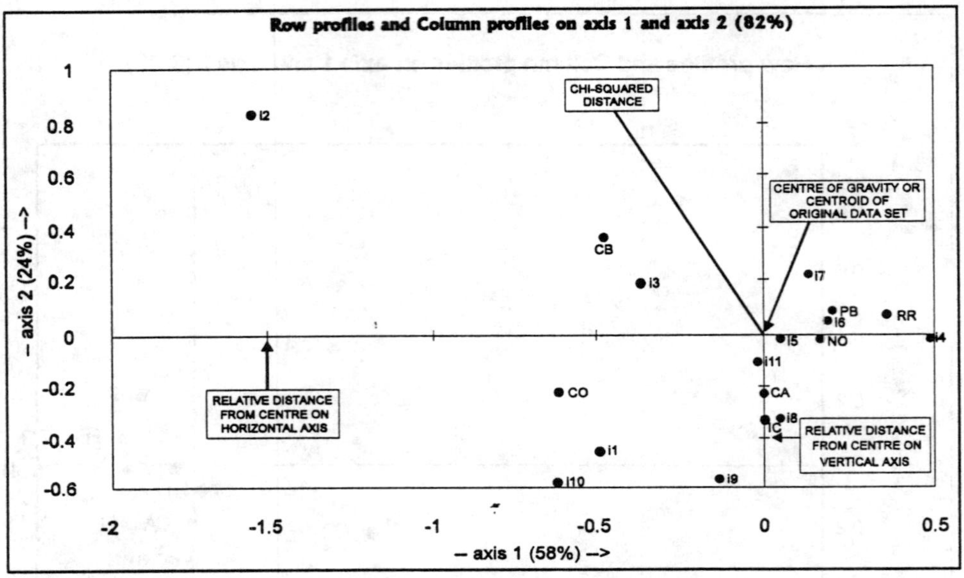

Figure 5.20: The perceptual map with the intercept, axes and distances explained

From Figure 5.19, it is possible to see that some of the themes and participating enterprises may be conveniently grouped together. For example the two themes CB and CO are to the left of the intersection of the axes, and the themes RR, PB and NO are all to the right of the axes. The two themes of change in the business processes and contribution to the business may well represented technological issues and it is not surprising that these themes lie in proximity on the horizontal axis to another. The industries that fall close to this area on the graph may well be described as having a technological focus. In a similar way reducing of risk, productivity and new opportunities may be described as performance issues, so it is not surprising that these themes lie in proximity on the horizontal scale to one another. The fact that these themes are spread on the vertical axis does not detract from their grouping on the horizontal axis. The industries that fall close to this area on the graph could be described as having a performance orientation. These two new variables also represent a bipolar dimension with technology as one end of the scale and performance on the other. These two variables have been defined for the horizontal axis, which may offer some insight into the way that organisations may approach the way they identify benefits derived from the placement of an IT investment. Figure 5.21 shows the grouping of these themes on the horizontal axis.

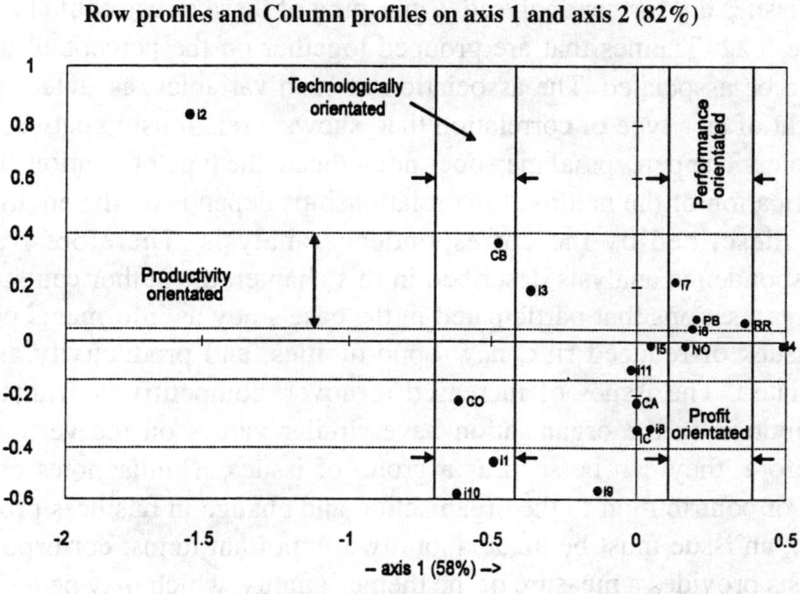

Figure 5.21: The perceptual map with horizontal and vertical axis defined

With regards the vertical axis, the themes of CO, CA and IC are grouped together. In fact they constitute a cluster, which on the horizontal axis CA and IC are close together about the origin, and on the vertical axis are closer together but away from the origin. The three themes of competitive advantage, increased turnover and contribution to the organisation may all be described as profitability issues and it is not surprising that these themes lie in proximity to one another. The enterprises that fall close to this area on the graph could be described as having a profit focus. Figure 5.21 shows the grouping of these themes on the vertical axis (dotted lines). At the other end of the vertical axis there are the themes RR, PB and CB. The projection of these themes onto the vertical axis may seem to be close; therefore, there seems to be an association between them on this dimension. All three issues of reducing of risk, productivity and change in the business processes are productivity issues and industries in this area could be described as productivity oriented. This provides the second bipolar dimension or vertical axis.

All these issues seem to be in close proximity and seem to be associated. If these issues are further analysed, a grouping of these issues could be seen in Figure 5.22. Themes that are grouped together on the perceptual map are said to be associated. The association of such variables, as stated, may be thought of as a type of correlation that shows a relationship between these variables. The perceptual map does not indicate the type of relationship. The specification of the nature of the relationships depends on the environment being described by the correspondence analysis. Therefore from the correspondence analysis described in this chapter, the author can state that the organisations that participated in the case study as informants perceive the issues of reduced risk, new opportunities, and productivity as being associated. The issues of increased turnover, competitive advantage and contribution to the organisation have similar values on the vertical axis. Therefore, they can be seen as a group of issues. Similar notes could be made of contribution to the organisation and change in business processes. Again, an issue must be made about two important items: correspondence analysis provides a measure of the themes quality, which may be defined as the extent to which variables are well represented in the number of dimensions being presented. The quality rating for new opportunities is low; therefore, it is not necessarily close to the horizontal axis, since it is actually on a two-dimensional piece of paper. The other two variables of reduced risk and productivity have different vertical axis scores. The scores suggest that reduced risk and productivity be treated differently. This perceptual map shows both reduced risk and productivity as part of the productivity and performance issues. This corresponds with the idea that organisations will want to improve their productivity by increasing their performance. This idea will be reflected in their IS policy.

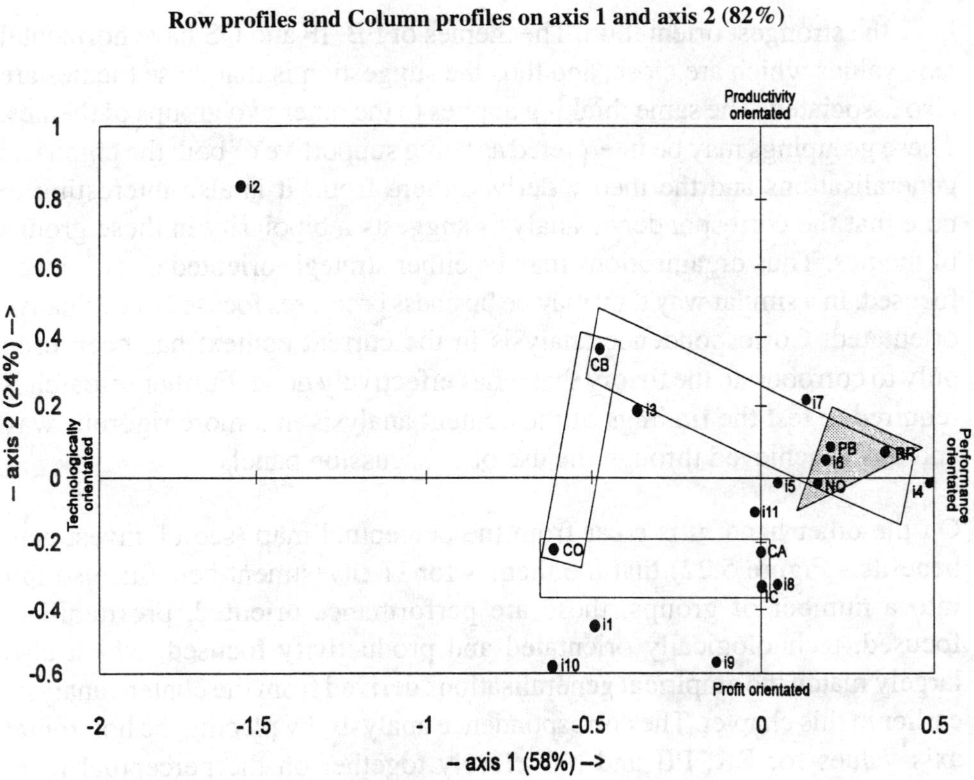

Figure 5.22: The perceptual map showing the horizontal and vertical axes

Again, in the same way as the themes have been grouped, so the participating organisations may be grouped. For the purposes of this research, however, this is not of much value and therefore has not been done.

Interpretation of the correspondence analysis results

It is clear from the perceptual map (IT investment drivers - Figure 5.14) that the themes could be grouped together into a number of groups, i.e., efficiency focus, business processes, strategic orientation and evaluation orientation, which largely match the empirical generalisations derived from the content analysis earlier in this chapter (see the groupings added in Figure 5.14). The correspondence analysis, by placing the horizontal and vertical axis values for MD and OS suggests that these activities are associated. These two themes have the strongest orientation. The themes of FB, IF and QS have horizontal axis values which are close, and thus the suggestion is that these themes are also associated. The same thinking applies to the other two groups of themes. These groupings may be interpreted as being supportive of both the empirical generalisations and the theory derived there from. It is also interesting to note that the correspondence analysis suggests a bipolarity in these groups of themes. Thus organisations may be either strategi- oriented or efficiency focused. In a similar way they may be business processes focused or evaluative orientated. Correspondence analysis in the current context has been used only to corroborate the theory that it has effectively done. Further research is required to test the findings of the content analysis in a more rigorous way and this is achieved through the use of a discussion panel.

On the other hand, it is clear from the perceptual map (see IT investment benefits - Figure 5.22) that the themes for IT investment benefits also fall into a number of groups, these are performance-oriented, profitability-focused, technologically orientated and productivity focused, which also largely match the empirical generalisations derived from the content analysis earlier in this chapter. The correspondence analysis, by placing the horizontal axis values for RR, PB and NO closely together on the perceptual map, suggests that these activities are associated. These three themes have the strongest orientation. The themes of CB and CO have horizontal axis values that are close, and thus, these themes are also associated. The same thinking applies to the other two groups of themes. These groupings may be interpreted as being also supportive of both the empirical generalisations and the theory derived there from (as was also stated previously). It is also interesting to note that the correspondence analysis suggests a bipolarity in these groups of themes. Thus organisations may be either productivity-orientated or profit oriented. In a similar way, they may be technologically oriented or performance focused—this bipolarity will thus apply while reviewing IT investment benefits. Correspondence analysis in the current context has been used only to help corroborate the theory that was formed. By the explanations above, it can be noted that this type of analysis has effectively done so. Further research is required to test the findings of the content analysis in a more rigorous way; this is achieved through the use of a focus group. The chi-square hypothesis of independence between rows and columns was rejected for IT investment drivers. This could be interpreted that there is a relationship between the industries and the drivers for IT investment. The hypothesis of independence between rows and columns for IT investment benefits cannot be rejected.

SUMMARY

In Chapter 5, the analysis of the case studies was described and it was shown how empirical generalisations and a theory were developed. The use of correspondence analysis to help authenticate the empirical generalisations and the theory was shown. The correspondence analysis was also used to gain a greater understanding of the data. This was specifically achieved by looking carefully at the configuration of the data on a perceptual map that helps to verify and assign meaning to relationships and associations between the data points. It also showed the vertical and horizontal axes to be interpreted.

The next two chapters address how the empirical generalisations were tested using a focus group and practitioners.

ENDNOTES

[1] The informants for the case studies have indicated these aspects to affect productivity.

[2] Other issues mentioned by informants only once or twice and that are therefore excluded from the list of themes for Figure 5.1 include industry drivers, IS developments in the industry forcing organisations to invest in IT, the development of their own systems, copying of IT investments, and service level agreements that ensure that the organisation keeps up to date with their IT.

[3] These drivers were given concise or appropriate names, describing the expression used by the informants and sometimes they should not be interpreted as literally meaning what the words used (e.g., business modelling could be interpreted as redesigning or designing business processes, turning these into computerised processes, and the informants felt that these should be treated as a separate theme and not grouped with other drivers).

[4] Other issues mentioned by informants only once or twice and that are therefore excluded from the list of themes for Figure 5.2 include organisationsal culture, organisational structure, help for the organisation to achieve its objective, acceptance of IT, and how time of the employees could be better spent.

[5] The author believes that the learning process could be defined as a series of activities involved in improving performance in order for the organisation to benefit from a higher level of understanding.

[6] IT investment targets are identified in this book as seven themes (e.g., management decisions) that could be used as a reason for IT investments (Figure 5.6).

[7] Four organisations were visited and the results were discussed with them (Chapter 6). A follow-up study should be conducted to find if all the organisations were portrayed correctly on these figures.

REFERENCES

Bailey K.D. (1987) *Methods of Social Research*, The Free Press, New York.

Berelson *cited* in Kroppendorff K. (1980) Content analysis, Sage Publications, Beverley Hills.

Huberman A.M. & Miles M.B.(1994), in Handbook of Qualitative Research, edited by Denzin N.K. & Lincoln Y.S. Sage London.

Green P.E., Carmone Jr. F.J. and Smith S.M. (1989). *Multidimensional scaling,* Allyn & Bacon, Boston, Mass.

Greenacre M.J. (1984). *The theory and applications of Correspondence* Analysis, Academic Press, London.

Kerlinger F.N. (1969). *Foundations of Behavioural Research*, Holt Rhinehart and Winston, London.

Nachmias C. & Nachmias D. (1989). *Research methods in the Social Sciences,* Edward Arnold, London

Miles M.B & Hubermann A.M. (1984).*Qualitative data analysis: A sourcebook of new methods*, Sage Publications, London.

Popper K. (1972). *cited* in Harre R. *The Philosophies of Science: an introductory survey*, Oxford University Press.

Chapter Six
Presentation of the Theoretical Conjecture to a Focus Group and Practitioners: Refinement of Conclusions

Introduction

The chapter discusses the presentation of the theoretical conjecture to a focus group and a series of practitioners. The aim of the chapter is therefore to describe feedback obtained from the focus group and the practitioners (IT people and consultants) and their reaction to the theoretical conjecture and the models suggested by the research. The reactions of these expert informants are also interpreted and the conclusions of the research refined. It has been done as a cross validation procedure.

The reasons for using a focus group

In order to verify whether the theory derived from the evidence collected during the case study phase of the research commands support from practitioners in business, it was decided to discuss the theoretical conjecture and the models with expert informants. The focus group also provided an opportunity to falsify the empirical generalisation that the author generated. The summaries of the empirical generalisations were faxed to them for perusal (Chapter 5) and they subsequently met at the University of the Witwatersrand to discuss ideas arising from the research. The researcher started off these discussions, but he allowed the people to freely discuss the ideas generated by the research, because he did not want to influence the outcome of the focus groups. Notes were taken, summarised, and subsequently drafted into the dissertation.

The focus groups consisted of practitioners, academics and consultants. The group consisted of several persons, i.e., a person who previously had more than 30 years experience as an IT manager and who presently acts as an independent consultant; a senior IT manager with more than 20 years of experience in one of the biggest banking groups in South Africa; a chartered accountant with more than 15 years of experience in auditing IT systems and organisations; a University Professor (from another university) with more than 15 years of experience as a consultant and has attended conferences by invitation worldwide; an IT Head of Department in a major banking group in South Africa; and a gentleman who previously worked as a bank manager for more than ten years and now acts as administrative manager for a group that uses IT widely and is responsible for the IT section. Other people who were part of the focus group were financial managers with lots of experience and who are responsible for IT purchases, IT managers and accountants responsible for IT systems of organisations.

The three models, shown previously in Figures 5.5, 5.6 and 5.7, presented the IT investment process (historically and proposed) and benefits identification and development process were discussed. The empirical generalisations relate to the following IT investment issues that are:

- Drivers for IT investment (targets).
- Response to the opportunity created.
- Achieving and evaluating IT investment targets.
- Benefits to be realised with the assistance of the IT investment.

The people for the focus group agreed to critically review the document and the models that were created. The review was in the form of a discussion. As a result of the feedback obtained from these individuals, minor changes were made to a couple of the suggestions.

Feedback from the focus group

The focus group informants were from the financial industry, the electronics industry, the transport industry and the mining industry. A couple of outside experts were also approached to participate as part of the discussion panel.

Results of the focus group discussion

Empirical generalisation 1:

- *IT investments occur as a result of targets identified by top management because of one or more drivers classified in Figures 5.1 and 5.6 and 6.1.*

The focus group agreed that the principle should apply as is it was stated. Although the author explained the term *budget* to the budget group, they suggested that the term *budget constraints* would rather be used because it suits the situation better.

Empirical generalisation 2:

- *The organisation's response to the opportunity for the assessment of the effectiveness of IT investments is influenced by the themes affecting the IT investment process. Both tangible and intangible benefits are included. The precise themes directly dictate the evaluation process that will be used. Tangible benefits will be measured financially and intangible benefits will be measured qualitatively.*

Again, the focus group agreed that the process should stay the same. The group suggested also that more people should be involved with IT investment and that the term *stakeholders* would be a better description to describe involvement of the people with all IT investments. They also suggested that the term was more in line with industry's expectations and Figure 6.2 was thus changed accordingly. It was suggested that the term *stakeholders* should be defined. They suggested that the following wording be used: Stakeholders could be described as all people involved with the use and development (including relevant managers) of IT.

Empirical generalisation 3:

- *The decision to invest resources into IT is taken with the help of action plans (a strategy) aimed at achieving the IT investment targets like efficiency (quality of service), improving business processes (modelling), etc. with attention to detail concerning the ability of managers to review and update these action programmes in conjunction with subordinates (see Figure 5.6 and Figure 6.1).*

The focus group agreed that the procedure above that should be followed. They agreed that there should be a change in the terminology, i.e., *benefit* should be replaced by the word *outcome*, as some organisations might not use the word *benefit*. *Benefit identification* was changed to *outcome identification* and *review action programmes* to *achieve targets* and *agree on benefit standards* were changed to read *agree on outcome standards* because some organisations do not use benefit identification.

Empirical generalisation 4:

- *Attention is given to specification of benefit objectives (productivity, profitability, etc.), realisation of IT benefits and to communication with staff members at all levels of the hierarchy of the organisation (see Figure 5.7 and Figure 6.2).*

The word benefit was replaced by the word outcome in Figure 6.2 (compare Figure 5.7 and Figure 6.2). They also agreed that the benefits identified could be replaced by other organisations by themes that they want to use. A note was made of it (Figure 6.2).

The focus group was satisfied with the findings in general. However, they agreed that the first model (Figure 6.1) needed some adapting. A revision period of three to six months might not always fit in with the current revision plans of the organisation; they, therefore, agreed that it should be readjusted to read *appropriate time interval*. The change they suggested was because project life span might be over either shorter or longer periods and organisations might use another timespan for investigation.

One of the focus group members was excited about the association between reduced risk, new opportunities and productivity. He stated that it was suspected by industry, but the idea was rarely presented formally by most of the studies. He further noted that the contribution of the finding would be appropriate to justify future research to investigate suggestions by the present study.

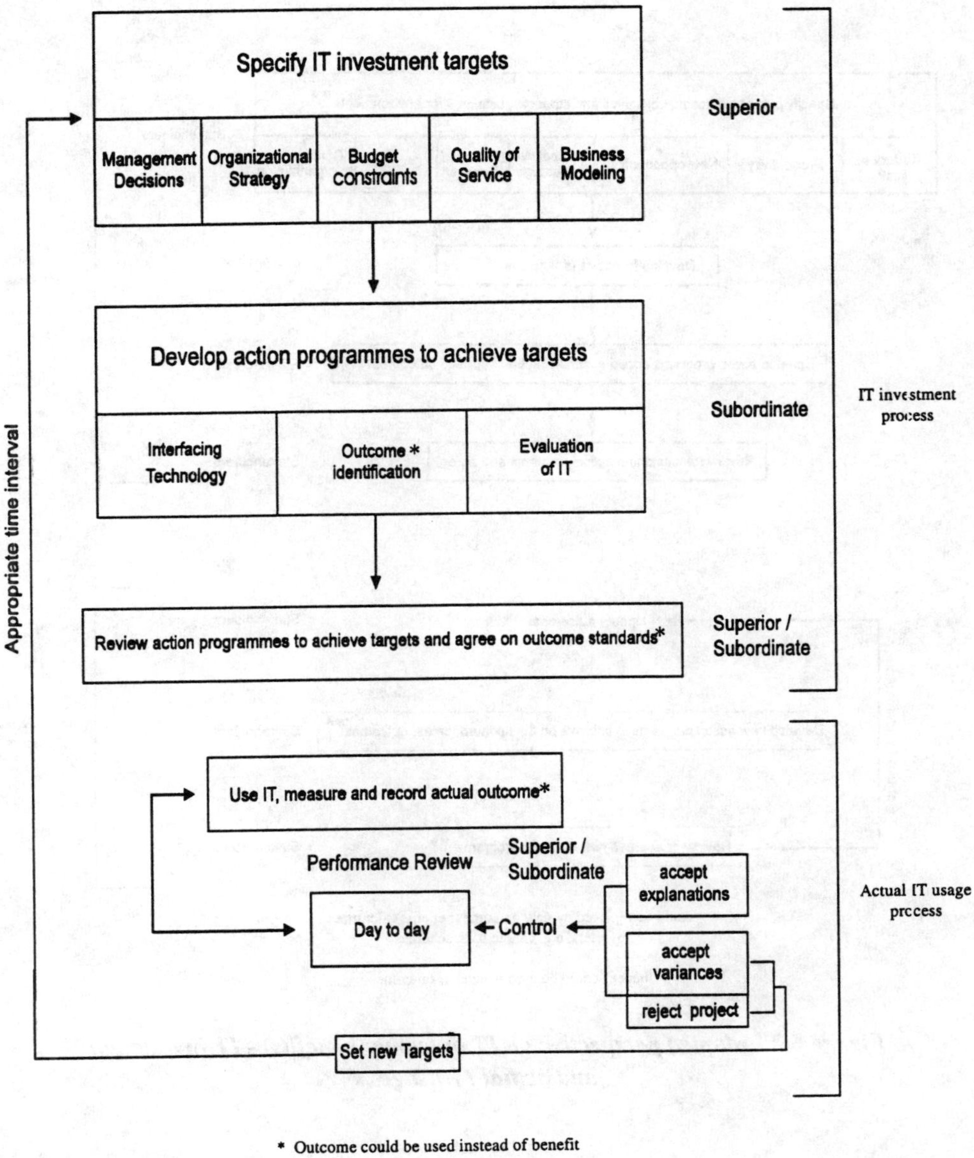

Figure 6.1: The Proposed IT investment process and usage model with the suggested changes made

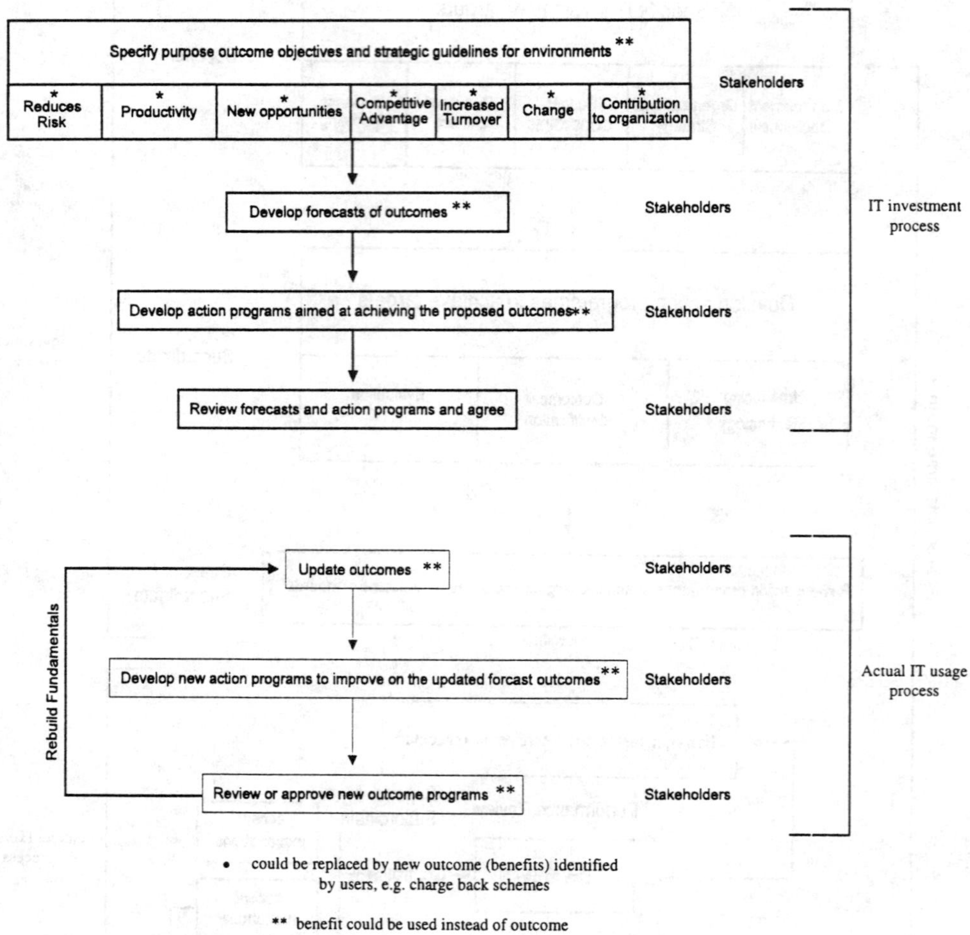

Figure 6.2: Adopted perspective on IT outcome (benefits) - IT investment and actual IT usage

In general it could be noted from the discussion by the focus group that complex systems (organisations) show certain common behaviours and should be studied as a unit. The interesting part could be to study holistically the interaction between the IT and the other components within the same system. The group also discussed the theoretical conjecture. It was accepted as a useful theory by the group with no changes.

Therefore, no changes were required by the focus group of the theory created by the study. The theory accepted was thus:

IT investments occur as a result of targets identified by top management because of one or more drivers classified in Figure 6.1. These targets are developed into action plans in conjunction with subordinates and the plans are regularly reviewed.

The organisation's response to the opportunity for the assessment of the effectiveness of IT investment is influenced by the themes affecting the IT investment process as shown in Figure 6.2. The decision to invest resources into IT is taken with the help of action plans (a strategy) aimed at achieving the IT investment targets like efficiency (quality of service), improving business processes (modelling), etc. with attention to detail concerning the ability of management to update the action programmes.

Attention is given to the specification of outcome (benefit) objectives (productivity, profitability, etc.), realisation of IT outcome (benefits) and to communication with staff members at all levels of the hierarchy of the organisation. It is important to include all outcome (benefits), both tangible and intangible. Evaluation is conducted regularly for control purposes and the result of the evaluation may be one of the three outcome described in Figure 6.2. When the evaluation dictates a change to the system, outcome (benefit) profiles and programmes are updated and rebuilt as per Figure 6.2.

Practical management guidelines

As well as developing a theory as to how IT investment should be formulated, developed and evaluated, the research also has an objective—to create a series of management guidelines which will assist organisations in applying formal procedures when making any IT investments.

These guidelines have been developed from the theory and the models as well as from the results of all the different evidence-gathering activities undertaken by the author during the research. The ten principles so developed reflect all the key elements of the theory further developed into the form of practical management guidelines for IT investment.

In order for an IT investment to be formulated, implemented and evaluated in an effective format, the practitioner should:

1. Clarify top management targets. IT investments occur as the result of targets identified by top management. It means the organisation must look for one or more drivers that could be classified into one or more of the themes identified. The IT investment are thus not just easy internal targets for IT investments. There is evidence from nearly all the case studies to support the principle and it is in line with the studies of Earl (1992), Ward *et al.* (1996), Hitt & Brynjolfson (1996).

2. Get to know the drivers for IT investment well and what is likely to change in the short to medium term. It involves monitoring the basic economics of the industry, the industry's technology, the competition and developments in the IT industry. It would probably require the setup of a scanning group and incorporation of these reports into the IT investment planning process. The Serenity Bank and MITD are examples of organisations that apply the guideline. The outward process is supported by the work of Farbey *et al* (1995a).

3. Develop IT investment targets that are clear and understandable to all parties in the organisation. Subordinates that develop the action plans and test the IT should know what they need to do and what managers expect from them. The Serenity Bank and the MITD apply the guideline in detail.

4. Outcome (benefit) objectives should be spelled out clearly because they would affect the action plans that would ensure the success of the IT investment. It applies to both tangible and intangible outcome (benefits). All these should be in a format to ensure that everything is running smoothly and that no one will be able to state that they did not know what to do at any stage. Documentation should thus be available at all times. The Serenity Bank, Fast Couriers and Freddies Instruments are organisations that ensure the outcome (benefit) objectives are understood by their IT staff.

5. Keep the organisation's IT investment objectives and IT strategy in the consciousness of the staff as much as possible. Match all IT investment proposals to IT investment strategy and action plans. Make sure that all persons measuring and noting outcome (benefits) have a known and reliable performance index or measure with which to evaluate each outcome (benefit) type, both tangible and intangible. Again, the Serenity Bank and MITD are examples. Deitz & Renkema (1995) support the principle in their study.

6. Determine the attitude of top management. Is management sensitive to IT investment processes and its potential? It implies that managers are fully aware of the IT strategy and targets. Does the rest of the organisation have the skills to make the IT investment process work? Freddies Instruments is an example of this. They invested into one large system, but are now faced with a major task of investing into more IT. Furthermore, the work by Lubbe (1994) and Kaye *et al* (1995) support the principle.

7. The organisation must ensure that staff involvement receives the required attention. It may be achieved by ensuring that everybody is fully briefed. Specific thought must be given to training schedules. Training should be part of the IT investment costs. The most impressive application regard was in Serenity Bank. They made provision and ensured that their staff received the training necessary to ensure a smooth IT investment process.

8. Develop adequate support facilities that can handle a wide range of problems. The basis should be a partnership between all the stakeholders in such a way that a two-way communication channel exists between groups of stakeholders who must ensure that the IT investment process is successfully completed. Earl (1992) conducted work on the topic while BAS supports the principle.

9. Look for IT investment targets across a wide range of issues, especially in areas that relate directly to the IT strategy and organisational strategy. IT outcome (benefits) should be high on the lists of targets searched for. Regular evaluation needs to be conducted to ensure outcome (benefit)

realisation. The Serenity Bank applies all of these mentioned in the guideline. The works by Butler-Cox (1990) also support the principle.

10. Adequately staff the IT investment process and implementation with suitably trained and experienced personnel. Such staff must have both the skills of general managers as well as be fluent in IT. Carlson & McNurlin (1992) support the principle. There is also evidence that the Mining Information Technology Division and Serenity Bank ensured that they have adequate staff to apply it.

It is clear that such a practical management guideline requires considerable time and resources. Also top managers need to be committed to ensure that all concerned promptly comply with these guidelines, and that certain people do not get side-tracked by departmental issues. In applying the guidelines suggested, many organisations would have to face management change of a cultural change exercise.

Results of the presentation to the practitioners

Senior practitioners from four of the original case study organisations were approached to discuss the theory, models and the practical management guidelines. The correspondence analysis figures (Figures 5.15 and 5.22) were also shown to these senior practitioners in order to validate the results of the content analysis for IT investment drivers and IT outcome (benefits) identified.

Organisation #1

The presentation was to one of the organisations in the transport industry that participated in the original case study. The informants indicated that they strongly agree with the findings and recommendations of the research and indicated that they would like to apply some (if not all) of the new ideas. They investigated all the aspects mentioned and noted that the study was what they needed to help them manage their IT and they regarded the study as very useful.

The study addressed their questions regarding IT investment. They requested permission to use the models that were adapted and noted that they would give further feedback to the author in due course. It could be possible to use the organisation as a model, apply all the aspects and conduct a separate case study on the application of the study findings. The informant invited the author for another session as they are in the process of studying the models in more details and would like advice on how to apply some of the processes identified. They point out that it would need a lot of training and education, because not all top managers were convinced of the importance of IT investment. They were prompted to look at their position on the correspondence analysis grid and were happy with it, indicating that it is where they would place their organisation.

Organisation #2

The second respondent stated that they were satisfied with the findings. They were in the process of changing the way they address the IT investment process in the organisation. The principles presented to them were issues that they felt should be addressed but were not always the case. They did believe however that it would not too difficult to achieve the suggested type of management thinking in their organisation.

The practitioner felt that the little progress they were making, the case study done and aspects mentioned in the study would help them to improve on the way they handle all IT investments. He felt that the principles discussed during the presentation were very useful and that some of the aspects had already been incorporated into the organisation's own IT investment procedures.

Organisation #3

The third practitioner was also positive about the findings of the research and the fact that they could make use of it. They noted that their position on the correspondence analysis figure was the right one for their organisation and industry. They also noted that they were employing most of the principles listed in the models (Chapter 5). IT investment, it seems, has been successful in their organisation despite the recognition that they need to improve their procedures. The study, according to them, was a firm attempt to do it. They wanted time to study these processes and apply those they were not doing.

They claimed that their staff would welcome their organisation formally adopting an IT investment process as described in the research study findings.

Organisation #4

The fourth practitioner was also complimentary about the findings. In fact, he indicated that the study brought out aspects to which more attention should be paid in his organisation. He stated that the place of his organisation and industry were also plotted 'correctly' and that it was a promising study because it highlighted aspects that bigger organisations tend to accept as normal. He said that the human aspect should be highlighted. He also mentioned that the practical guidelines proposed should be a useful framework for his organisation.

SUMMARY

There are numerous opportunities for IT investment exercises. A seamless approach to formulating and implementing IT investment programmes is important. The theory suggested by the case study research is perceived to be useful; the theory suggests a list of principles that will assist organisations in achieving success with their formulation, implementation and evaluation of IT investment programmes.

ENDNOTES

[1] The focus group discussed arguments for and against the use of the word *outcome* instead of benefit to indicate a stream of improvements and eventually decided that the two concepts have similarities. The author, however, decided that he would incorporate the word *benefit* next to the word outcome in brackets to accommodate the suggested change and for organisations who only use one of the words.

REFERENCES

Butler-Cox Foundation (1990)."Getting value from Information Technology", *Research Report 75*, June, London.

Carlson W. & McNurlin B. (1992) "Basic Principles For Measuring IT value", *I/S Analyzer*, 30(10), 1 - 13.

Deitz R.M.H. & Renkema T.J.W. (1995).: "Planning and justifying investments in Information Technology: A framework with case study illustrations", *Proceedings of the 2nd Henley Conference on the Evaluation of IT Investments,* Henley Management College, Henley, UK, 28 - 41.

Earl M.J. (1992). "Putting IT in its place: a polemic for the nineties", J*ournal of Information Technology*, No 7, 100 - 08.

Farbey B., Land F. & Targett D. (1995). A taxonomy of information systems applications: the benefits evaluation ladder, *European Journal of Information Systems,* No 4, 41 - 50.

Hitt L.M & Brynjolfson E. (1996). Productivity, Business Profitability, and Consumer Surplus: Three Different Measures of Information Technology Value ,*MIS Quarterly*, June, 121 - 141.

Kaye G.R., Hinton C.M. & Armstrong S. (1995). "The Hidden Investment in IT: Dependency, Legacy and Heritage", *Proceedings of the 2nd Henley Conference on the Evaluation of IT Investments*, Henley Management College, Henley, UK, 249 - 259.

Lubbe S.I. (1994). *The impact of Information Technology* (IT) *on the financial performance of organisations in a developing country*, M.Com.-Thesis, UCT, Cape Town.

Ward J. Taylor P. & Bond P. (1996). "Evaluation and realisation of IS/IT Benefits: an empirical study of current practices", *European Journal of Information Systems*, 4, 214 - 225.

Chapter Seven
Conclusions: Limitations of the Research and Some Issues for Further Research

Introduction

The aim of the research was to investigate, to develop a theory, and to ground the theory concerning these issues:

How organisations in developing countries identify IT investments;

How organisations measure the impact of IT investments on the performance of organisations;

How the process of IT investment operates in an organisation; and,

Which criteria are used to evaluate the IT investment projects.

Conclusions

The conclusions of the research are considered under the headings described above.

How developing countries' organisations identify IT investments

Organisations sometimes identified IT investments as flashes of commercial insight and sometimes they identified an IT investment target because of some drivers like a management decision, budgetary constraints, quality of service or business modelling. These drivers were identified, an investment decision made and action programmes set to reach the IT investment target.

It can be concluded that organisations have to be more systematic about the identification of investments. They need to identify reasons (drivers) for the IT investment and then develop action programmes to achieve these targets.

How organisations measure the impact of IT investments on organisational performance

Most of the organisations conducted an informal assessment of the impact of IT investment. They regarded the impact as part of the outcome (benefits) they gained from doing the IT investment. Some organisations, for instance, noted the increase of productivity of their employees. It could be part of the drive to allow their staff to spent more productive time in front of the computer. Another factors that were measured by the organisations were increased turnover measured in the form of a percentage.

It can be recommended that specific target for measurement should be developed, performance reviews completed and reports given to management. Action should then be taken in the following format, e.g., the variance should be accepted and the IT investment should continue; or the variance should be accepted, but new targets should be set for the IT investment or lastly drastic action could be taken whereby the organisation rejects the IT investment totally and starts a new IT investment.

Formulation of IT investments in organisations

It is clear from the research that setting action plans for IT investment is not an easy matter to formulate and to implement. Opportunities for proper IT investment strategies are not always obvious; what appears to be a possible action plan for IT investment sometimes amounts to nothing, or is too complicated or too expensive to implement. How to accommodate IT investment action plans into the organisation's current IT strategy is not always easy. For this reason, it is important to have a set of explicit guidelines.

Key among these guidelines is the idea of drivers that could act as a reason for IT investment in a variety of ways. It is crucial for any organisation to be aware of these drivers and how they change. Environmental scanning could support the drivers and subsequent action plans.

These action plans and environmental scanning should be reviewed and the standards should be agreed upon. It should be done effectively and relatively quickly. All these are listed as part of the practical management guidelines in Chapter 6.

Which criteria are used to evaluate the IT investment projects?

Organisations claim to use a variety of criteria to evaluate the IT projects. Most of the organisations do not use a specific evaluation method but a combination of visual processes to evaluate the IT investment. Some of these criteria involve outcome (benefits) that organisations identifies like new opportunities, competitive advantage that the organisation can achieve by placing the IT investment, new business opportunities, etc.

Action programmes should be developed to evaluate the IT investment and achieve the targets spelled out by the stakeholders. It can be suggested that all interested parties, i.e., stakeholders, should be involved in the process. It starts with the specification of outcome (benefit) objectives through meetings. Stakeholder involvement, of course, also has begun through the action plan formulation for the IT investment process proposed by management. Where possible, an attitude of communication partnership should be put between all the interested parties within the stakeholder group. However, the senior person in the group should be the representative of the group and the owner of the IT investment. The key ingredients to make it work are to develop specifications for outcome (benefit) forecasts and training. Both of these are ongoing commitments across the whole life cycle of the IT investment, and they must be properly planned for and accounted for into the IT investment.

In addition, successful realisation of IT outcome (benefits) relies on careful planning and reviewing, and organisations should be spending more time and money on the planning of the realisation of IT outcome (benefits) process. IT investment and outcome (benefit) realisation cannot succeed without appropriate staffing and it requires a lot of detailed planning and precise execution. It is a costly process which organisations should only undertake after appropriate consideration.

The above research questions were also answered by the models shown in Figure 5.6 (6.1) and Figure 5.7 (6.2).

Limitations of the research

As was mentioned before, the aim of the research was to investigate, to develop a theory and to ground a theory of why and how organisations invest in IT. Once it was decided upon, the research set out to assess the overall situation and certain recommendations were made. Why and how questions require a primarily qualitative approach to the research. Qualitative research is especially subject to bias. Being aware of it, the author tried to minimise the bias through the use of triangulation. However, bias cannot be totally discounted.

The technique of content analysis, which is an important element of the research, relies on the principle of manifest content categories. These categories are concept groups that the researcher nominates. The author chose these groups and the choice was subjective. It could be possible for a different researcher to choose different manifest content categories and thus derive a different thesis or theory. The author was aware of the subjectivity and looked at the evidence in as many ways as possible, and thus attempted to reduce the bias.

The sample used for the survey research could be challenged on the grounds of its representativeness of the universe of IT investment. There is no way of truly knowing how representative such a sample really is. The number of organisations used (20) could also be queried but 20 was used because it was deemed to be a practical number for the purposes of a research program and because a reasonably widespread number of opinions could be obtained. However, in discussion with a number of industry observers, the author concluded that the informants probably constitute a reasonable sample of the universe of those experienced in the formulation and implementation of IT investments. Although the sample could be regarded as reasonable, the complexity of the issues at stake necessitated a follow-up of the research to test the conclusions. A follow-up study with a larger sample and a questionnaire could help to generalise the study to other industries and organisations.

As previously explained, the author decided to focus on organisations of which it was reasonable to expect would go about the formulation and implementation of their IT investments and IT outcome (benefits) realisation in the most effective way they can. Of course, it meant that no attempt was made to learn from situations in which IT investment and IT outcome (benefits) realisations had failed. The main reason for it is that there is often much to be learned from situations of failure and there is often much to learn from observing success. In any event it is difficult enough for the researcher to be taken into the confidence of individuals in an organisation when they are describing a situation in which they think they have not made mistakes.

The final validation procedure is regarded as useful in that it confirmed the usefulness of the theory to practitioners.

In defence, we understood although there are a number of areas where the techniques used are vulnerable, the author was aware of these limitations and took reasonable precautions to help minimise possible misunderstandings and misrepresentations.

In the final analysis, it is not possible to tell in the short term the differences between good and bad research. However, the findings of good research will survive over time and the findings of bad research will be quickly forgotten.

Finally, the research programme concludes with a set of principles which may be applied in practical management guidelines, and which actual practitioners have stated to be useful to their organisation. It provides a major justification for the research, i.e., that the results of the research have produced a theory and a set of principles that may have been developed into a management programme which is of specific use to the business community.

A general issue

Generally a great deal of interest has been shown in the subject of IT investment and its evaluation. All the informants, consultants, academics, practitioners, etc. with whom the author had discussions throughout the research were very enthusiastic and helpful about the subject. Many of these informants were very pleased to be involved in research on the subject.

The results of the focus group discussions and the presentations to the practitioners also supported the view that a large number of organisations considered IT investment and outcome (benefits) identification to be an important issue. In fact, the situation may be seen to constitute two groups, one which is very large and quite enthusiastic, and one which is small and not very keen. Therefore, it is clear that IT investment evaluation and IT outcome (benefits) identification is likely to remain an important subject for practitioners, consultants and academics for quite some time into the future. The research is, however, an original approach to the assessment of the effectiveness of IT investment; no other similar research using such an approach exists. The research, however, did not address how to identify the different levels of IT investments or predict what outcome (benefits) could be derived form any IT investment. It is undoubtedly an area for future investigation.

It appears from the research that there is a trend towards combining the issues of formulation and implementation of IT investments and the identification of IT outcome (benefits) together, as effective IT investments will benefit from a seamless approach from start to finish. It is reflected in a generally higher level of awareness of organisations concerning the importance of IT investment.

Issues for further research

There are many opportunities for further research in the field of IT investment and IT outcome (benefits) identification. As previously suggested, the question of outcome (benefits) identification and the level any organisation would like to apply it deserves exploration. Also an area for research is to identify the different IT investments or to predict which outcome (benefits) could stem from a specific IT investment.

The research did not focus on industry sector, but rather attempted to look at a range of industries in order to establish general principles that might apply to all organisations. It would now be interesting to conduct research similar to the project on specific industries to see what issues are especially relevant to each individual industry sector. It would even be more interesting to compare these organisations in the same industry and see if it produces the same results as was for the industry.

As more and more organisations apply action plans for IT investments and IT outcome (benefit) realisation programme principles, the IT investment effectiveness will increase. It would be interesting to look at an organisation such as Serenity Bank who has an excellent record of IT investment planning and see if these principles apply, or if they applied in the past but are now evolved into something else.

Finally, a major opportunity for research exists in the field to ensure that the necessary attention is paid to the action programme in an organisation so that the programme would not simply be motherhood statements recited by all but followed by none.

APPENDIX A

Details of the Cases Conducted in IT-intensive Organisations

Imaginary names for all organisations in the case studies will be used because confidentiality was promised to all organisations. The data, however, is real.

Case Study 1: Educational:

Vision Training College

Introducing VTC

The Vision Training College's (VTC) is one of the larger black educational institutions in South Africa. VTC has seven distributed sites with their Head Office in Pretoria. Like all universities they are going through a period of transformation, the period (1989 - 1995) was not without turmoil and VTC was without a vice-chancellor for two years (late 1994 to early 1996). They are employing about 1,400 people. VTC was founded in 1982 and has five divisions: i.e., contact tuition, distance education, libraries, networks and an administration.

The main processes of VTC are to:

- supply quality lectures to their students;
- handle financial and other student matters;
- supply library services to their clients;
- do administrative duties concerned with an educational institution; and
- maintenance of equipment for VTC.

Strategy and Information Systems in VTC

Information technology and information systems in VTC are used extensively for student records and financial systems. The computer literacy level of academic staff and students are, however, below par and opportunities for computer use are limited because of the lack of computer facilities. VTC indicated that there is no strategic plan in place for the organisation and that it is difficult to invest in IT without any directive from top management. It is beyond the scope of this case study to attempt to describe the number of IT applications used by VTC. This case study limits itself to looking at some aspects of how IT investments are formulated, benefits of IT investments measured and how IT affects the organisation. VTC also realised that there could be a major shortage of young skilled black staff by the year 2000. They forecast that IT would have to enhance staff productivity where possible.

Information Technology in VTC

VTC started with a Wang computer system during the 1980's. This system was gradually upgraded to the present system consisting of IBM compatible machines and a UNIX-box. The UNIX system is used for the libraries, student records and financial systems. The parameters for IT had been laid down; i.e., they know of what IT is comprised.

IT is controlled by the Director of Networks on behalf of the Council of VTC. All distributed sites have a Network Administrator in charge of the site's IT. These administrators have, as part of their duties, been assigned the extra duty of support for all hardware on the site. Each distributed site has their own Novell network and this site forms part of the countrywide VTC network. Each department has at least one personal computer on each site. These computers are all connected to the Internet and have direct access to a laser printer.

The file-servers (486DXs) on each site are equipped with 32 megabytes of RAM and at least a 1-Gigabyte hard drive. The policy of VTC is to supply all staff with a 486DX 4-100 machine with 8 megabyte of RAM and a 540 megabyte hard drive, .28 SVGA monitor, mouse and Windows, while WordPerfect and Quattro Pro are standard software available to all staff.

MSWorks is used to teach the students utilising 486DX 4-66 diskless machines connected to the Novell network. The Administrative Division uses financial and other specialised software developed by similar institutions. Specialised software, like students' registration software were outsourced for developing purposes. PCs are maintained by VTC. IT has not been co-ordinated with other interfacing functions while IT does not have the influence for which VTC had hoped.

Plans, Budgets and the IT investment process

Assets are budgeted for and motivated by each Head of Department and approved by the Finance Department in the Administrative Division and finally the Council of the Organisation. The network's divisional budget at VTC is not large enough to enable the network's division to issue all staff at VTC with computers. VTC also stated that extensive business modelling should be performed to evaluate all alternatives before they invest any resources into IT. Plans and budgets are not exploded into the next level of detail for each functional head. The IT budget is only expressed in terms of resources (expense and asset) after an amount had been approved. The network's division should adapt to the changing environment but IT's growth might be too fast for them.

The main reason for placing an IT investment is because of a general upgrade of IT or because of staff that needs a personal computer. Each Head of Department distributes a standard form to their staff at each site (submissions do not have to be on this form;however, they should be well motivated). If a a staff member should need a personal computer, he would complete the form and indicate what type of software is needed. The Head of Department approves or rejects applications and sends the approved applications through to the Network's Division.

The Networks Division collates all these applications and, with the help of the Director of Finance, decides if the IT investments are approved. Staff members are allocated a computer without any direct input, because top management decides on the type of personal computer. Any deviation from the standard for IT must be especially motivated. Applications that were rejected could be submitted again during the next financial period. The IT budget was never calculated as a ratio.

Hidden costs are not included in any investment. Risks such as theft and damage to IT are experienced daily, but neither these nor business risks are included as part of the calculations of IT investment. IT investments are not tied to any strategic or investment strategies. Most IT investments are gut feeling investments. VTC, however, noted that IT investments cannot be divorced from organisational issues.

VTC noted that a need exists to consult users on what their needs are and by addressing this need VTC hopes to reduce IT investment mistakes made in the past. Software, especially academic software, needs to be evaluated before they invest in it. The Networks Department accepts an investment proposal by any department as an act of faith. Departments submitting the IT investment do not have to take responsibility for any IT investments allocated to them.

IT as organisational resource

There is another resource available to VTC, in addition to expenses and assets, which relates to the benefits a particular IT investment can yield. These benefits could help VTC to reach its goals; however, they are not measuring any benefits. They also do not know how to train staff to optimally use PCs and receive benefit from IT investments. VTC notes that the effect of culture affects any possible benefits they could have received because of the dis-enfranchised population they serve.

They are using their limited financial resources and should apply financial criteria. IT should supply information to management (management criteria) and should not affect the networks (technical criteria). VTC does not apply post-implementation evaluation.

SUMMARY

The case study has attempted to provide as brief insight into some of the issues, which an educational institution has to manage in the pursuit of IT, investments. The case study has looked at some of the issues which could be addressed when an IT investment had been placed at an educational institution of this size. Gaps in the system had not yet been addressed by VTC and should be kept in mind by them and by similar institutions.

Computer Training (CT)

Background to the Organisation

Computer Training (CT) was founded in January 1995 in the Goldfields[1]. CT has three departments, i.e., Administration, Financial and a Training section. They are the local franchisees for a well-known countrywide training organisation with their Head Office in Gauteng. The local organisation employs 33 people.

CTs biggest competitors in the Goldfields are Unischool, Academy of Learning[2], Free State Technikon, Welkom College and Vista University. CT, a new player in the field of education in the Goldfields, is struggling to settle down (they moved office three times). The strategic plan of CT is to provide excellent training to the community.

The main processes of CT are to provide training and support to their students. CT is happy with the communication between the IT people and the rest of the staff and students at CT; in fact, they stated that some of their student's organisations are basing their own organisational models on the model designed by CT.

Information Technology and organisational strategy

CT is part of a large organisation with a long tradition dating back many years. It has a high standing in the educational market that it has achieved through an organisational strategy established by their Head Office. According to the local representative of CT, they believe that they are offering a better service because they offer high quality lectures, a range of good courses using good techniques, and good lectures using good lecturers, enabling their students the opportunity to be employed.

Quality of lectures is important to CT and the organisation ensures quality through a system of management control. Another aspect of concern with quality is the importance placed on selecting the best lecturers for their classes. In the area of lecturing techniques, CT is concerned with remaining in the lead in applying technology. This is why they linked their IT and organisational strategy.

IT in the organisation

The IT costs have been fluctuating a lot because they did not know precisely how much hardware to invest in, but the IT costs have been in the region of R 1,280,000 per annum. CT noted that IT has fulfilled all promises. They have a definition for IT and claims that the manager agrees with this definition of IT. The manager controls IT. CT uses a 486 file server running a Novell network and using software and integrated packages developed inhouse.

All people working at CT, including managers, have received appropriate training to use computers and the information they generate. All maintenance of computers has been attended to; they are using maintenance contracts. They also noted that IT controls and regulates the organisation. CT stated that their business' operations would not have been possible without IT.

IT investment approach

The accountant for CT takes all decisions to buy assets while the manager of the organisation prepares the motivation. This motivation can be in any format, as long as it is well motivated. CT does not have any other investments at this stage, it will therefore be difficult to tie IT investments to any other investment. All possible IT projects are monitored carefully to tie in with all IT investments. The manager submits all IT investments while junior staff can propose an IT investment that will be considered if it is beneficial to the organisation. These proposals might be discussed in more detail with the proposer if CT thinks that it is worth it to invest the money in acquiring extra IT.

The manager and senior staff members will evaluate any IT investment and the accountant will approve it. They will not consider any portfolio approaches for any IT investment and are not concerned about the interfacing function as they think that their staff can handle all software. CT noted that IT costs are difficult to contain.

IT benefit and criteria applied to IT benefits

CT determines the effect of IT investment on how much their PCs are in use and how the amount of income they generated with their PCs. CT measures benefits in financial terms, e.g., increase on turnover. CT does not consider hidden costs to be part of their IT investment. Business risks have to be considered in such a way because some of their projects require more time on the IT and because they will loose business. CTs competitors are also a major problem because CT does not know how to handle strategic IT investments and will lose more business because of this. CT does not know how to handle IT investments in order to gain competitive advantage.

CT does not look at specific IT investments but calculate how much time was spent on their personal computers. They consider an increase in turnover as part of their financial criteria and would see if the IT investment fits in with their present budget. Management criteria are not considered at all, while development/technical criteria are applied in the sense that they ensure that the software and hardware compliment each other. All the criteria mentioned do not carry any weight. The most important reason for placing an IT investment is to increase their turnover. CT classifies IT costs according to their definition. They do not differentiate between the different IT investments, all are handled in the same way. CT does not perform any post implementation evaluation. CTs IT investment procedure allows enough freedom to invest in IT if the need arises.

SUMMARY

CT is worried about the effect of organisational culture on their IT investments. They also do not know how this culture will affect the link between their IT and organisational culture. The effect of advanced IT would be a constant worrying factor to them because it would affect their IT investments. CT would like to see what the key IT attributes are of similar organisations. They also need to keep up to date with technology on which they want to train their students for future employment opportunities. In order to do so, they feel that they should set up a special project for this.

Computer Training Bureau

Introduction

Computer Training Bureau (CTB) is a training organisation in Kroonstad (Free State). Their only competitors in Kroonstad are the local teachers' training college. CTB is the local franchisees of a national training centre training their students on the new technology with a staff of 4. The main process of CTB is to train students in the use of technology enabling them to apply for jobs. Their national TV advertisement claims that people will definitely get a job if they complete a course with CTB.

CTB has two departments, a training section and an administration department. CTB was started during the second half of 1995. The organisation is a closed corporation and is run by a manager. Because CTB does not have a large staff, they claim that they do not have problems with communications. CTB operates in an increasingly competitive market. Also, it must be noted that most of the South African population sensed the need to further their education. CTB is trying to ensure that they could fulfil this need and at the same time find their niche in the market.

IT and organisational strategy

IT has helped to determine their business strategy but they were not prepared to link it to any other investment strategy. The search for competitive advantage also plays a major role in CTB. The strategic plan of CTB is to become a profitable business by delivering good quality lectures to their students, allowing them to become proficient in the use of computers and other technology. CTB tried to ensure that their strategic plan would last for at least five years. They are planning a market research exercise to find their place in the educational market. CTB is scared that they started their business too soon without being able to estimate the probability of making a profit. Their IT strategy is set to enable CTB to reach its organisational goals but they had not considered all possible IT opportunities. CTB's fear is is that they might become more technically-oriented than business-oriented.

Information Technology in the organisation

CTBs architecture consists of a Pentium file server and 486 terminals while the manager controls all IT. All CTBs software are integrated packages, they do not use in-house developed software. All people working in the organisation have received appropriate training to use computers and the information they generate. IT is still under guarantee, but they will organise a maintenance contract if the guarantee expires.

They did not know about the existence of hidden costs, nor were they prepared to include it as a part of their IT investment. The ITs budget is R 240,000 per annum. CTB notes that IT makes a valuable contribution to their business. They have a definition for IT; during the compilation of this definition, their strategy was to get all staff members involved. The manager takes all decisions to buy assets. He and two of the staff members prepare all motivations for IT and other asset acquisitions.

Information Technology's effects on the business

All IT investments have been planned carefully because CTB does not want to over-invest in IT. The manager and his staff decide on the appropriateness of any IT investment. CTB is a small business and the policy is that everybody should be involved with the planning of all IT investments. CTB feels that as long as they can deliver a good service to their clients, they will not approach them for any advice on what the IT platforms should be. There are no standard formats for IT investment proposals, as long as they are well motivated. They evaluate all these investments themselves and approve the IT investments if the general consensus is that it is worthwhile to do the IT investment. CTB has not considered the use of the portfolio approach for their IT investments. They are not too concerned with the interfacing function, as they feel that they can use all software that they have on their fileserver.

ITs benefits are measured in turnover, how many students they could help and their turnover at the end of each month. Financial criteria are considered important as IT investments must fit in with their budget or proposed extension of services. They don't consider any management criteria at this stage. The development/technical criteria are used to ensure that IT investments should fit in with their present IT hardware and with the organisation's profile.

These criteria are not given a specific weight, but are rather weighed by means of a gut feeling. The most important reason for placing any IT investment is to increase their turnover. CTB does not differentiate between the different types of software and is happy with their present evaluation process. CTB also breaks down IT costs according to the definition supplied and is not concerned about doing any post-implementation evaluation. CTB feels that they have great freedom to respond to expectations because they are a small organisation. Threshold investments are handled as normal investments and they can take this decision instantly.

SUMMARY

CTB reaches all spheres of the South African population, but they feel that they were not yet able to combine culture and IT. The question they also feel should be addressed is whether they should concentrate on reaching intangible objectives rather than improvement of IT. While CTB feels that there are lots of opportunities to educate the population of Kroonstad and surrounding areas, care should be taken that IT expenses does not run away (overspending).

Case Study 2: Local Government:

Transitional Local Council (TLC)

Introduction and General Background

The Transitional Local Council (TLC) is over 100 years old and is a municipality in the Free State. TLC is a service organisation and most of their offices are in a brand new building. The TLC suffers from the water, electricity and rates boycott, initiated to force the previous regime to stop the apartheid policy and allow the people to govern (democracy).

All the previous local councils in the greater boundary have been amalgamated into a greater local council, the present TLC. The problems that the old local councils had were also inherited and are becoming a problem to solve these and deliver normal services to the people within the boundaries of the TLC.

TLC has eight different departments, some of them are finance, services and computers. TLC has more than 4,000 workers in their employment. Some of these employees will be retrenched as soon as the final amalgamation is completed. This makes people unsure of their jobs.

Strategy and Information Systems in the TLC

Information technology and information systems are used extensively within TLC. They are also selling computer services to smaller councils in the Free State. However, they are trying to discover if there are any other drivers that will help them finalise their IT strategy because they do not have a defined IT strategy at present. The strategy of the TLC is to deliver services to all people living within the municipal boundaries. The transformation process, however, could affect the strategic plans of the TLC.

The IT Department

TLC has 15 employees in the IT department; a deputy city-treasurer is in charge of the IT department. He has three system analysts who control data typists, a distribution unit for printouts, and some programmers. TLC noted that they do not know what to implement and plan regarding IT. They are not happy with the way the IT department looks presently but it might take some time to rectify because of the transformation process presently on the go. TLC stated that the communication between the IT department and other departments are satisfactory. They would also like to finalise their IT strategy and link it to the organisational strategy.

The IT department noted that their contribution is significant to TLCs normal business activities but other business managers do not agree with this statement. The contribution of IT is measured by monitoring all the input and output on a daily basis. Whether they laid down the parameters of IT was regarded as a difficult question because nobody has set boundaries for IT. The computers are decentralised but they have decided to centralise the IT services. The City Treasurer controls IT. They use a mainframe and normal PCs as terminals while cashiers use dumb terminals.

Plans and Budgets

The total budget for IT is R 500,000 to R 700,000 per annum. The deputy city-treasurer noted that they need to visit similar organisation's IT departments to measure their standing in their community. They also need to educate the City Council on what contribution IT could make to the daily processes at TLC. Plans and budgets are expressed in terms of expense and assets required. The IT department's budget is not calculated as a percentage of the total budget and this limits their flexibility. The City Council takes decisions to sell and buy assets, this includes IT. The motivation for these assets are prepared by each Head of Department that requires the asset.

The IT investment Process

Any staff member can approach their Head of Department to submit an IT investment project. The IT investment will be considered if the head of department feels it is worth it and if there are not important projects that should be considered. These IT investments might be discussed in more detail by the potential user or group of users if it was felt that this project has merit. The Head of Department will have the project re-reviewed and a decision will be made to either accept or reject an IT investment.

IT investment projects' presentation could be in any format, as long as it is well motivated. The assistant City-Treasurer will review the project, discuss it with the City Treasurer and if accepted will submit it as part of their budget for the next financial year. The final budget will serve before the City Council who will approve or reject the IT budget. Only IT investments that uses the same interfacing functions are considered because it makes it easier to train end-users and by saving them the problem of being scared of new software.

Most software bought might be changed to suit their software needs, but they try to run it with little changes to the original software. If TLC buys software from outside, they confirm that it includes training. Normally maintenance are included in all the contracts. If they notice a new product, they try and run it at the same time as their present system. If it fulfills a present need, they will buy it. Hidden costs are not considered at all. They do not consider risks of any kind when placing their IT investment. Because they try software/hardware out before they buy, they reduce the possibility of making any mistakes when placing an investment. IT investment decisions are not tied to any other investment strategies. TLC reviews new software in terms of ease of use or new functions needed (technically and nice to have); however, they do not calculate any cost-benefit or other ratios.

Benefits measured and criteria applied to IT investments

TLC measures complaints as part of a benefit measurement of their IT services. If they receive a lot of complaints about wait stages on the system, they know that they must improve their IT. If they receive no complaints, they know that they are on the right track. No post-implementation evaluation is done by the IT department or any of the users, nor does TLC know how to evaluate its IT initiatives.

Financial criteria are important, but are only considered if there is a budget cutback and they need to reduce IT investments. Management criteria are used if the software support decisions made by the City Council. Technical/development criteria are applied to see if the software can be used in conjunction with present software and if the hardware can cope with the software. No specific weight is applied to any of the criteria mentioned. TLC does not perform any post-implementation evaluation, because they do not know how to do it.

SUMMARY

The case study has attempted to provide a brief insight into some of the IT investment issues which a large local council has to manage. This they have to do because of their effort to pursue a suitable IT investment and benefit identification process. No financial ratios are being calculated and this needs to be addressed if TLC wants to implement an IT strategy. TLC needs to address how large administrative systems have been developed to accommodate their business and can reduce costs and maintain a high degree of consistency.

Local Services Council

Introducing Local Services Council (LSC)

To many, the word gold is synonymous with the Goldfields of the Free State. The LSC has therefore been founded in 1948 because of the discovery of gold in the Goldfields of the Free State. It has been awarded city status and has eight divisions (i.e., Management Services, Parks and Recreation, etc.). LSC is a local services council delivering municipal services to the people living within its boundaries.

LSC is also suffering because of a rates boycott by the majority of the people staying in one of the black townships. This boycott was initiated by the black political movements and they had not been able to convince the people to end the boycott. The municipality also has to make major repairs to its sewerage pipes, roads and electricity lines because of sinkholes that appears regularly because of mining operations. These unexpected expenses hamper their budget seriously.

LSC employs 1,500 people and they had the inevitable task of amalgamating all the local councils within the greater municipal borders. It is expected that there might be retrenchments because there are too many people on the payroll of LSC.

Strategy and IS

Information technology is used extensively within LSC. However, it is beyond the scope of this study to attempt to describe all of the IT applications used by LSC. This case study limits itself to looking at some aspects of how IT investments are formulated, benefits identified, and post-implementation evaluation of IT investments conducted.

The strategic plan of LSC is to deliver a good service to its people staying within the municipal boundaries. The main processes of LSC can be described as providing diverse services to the community within its boundaries. The IT manager noted that the information and organisational strategy are linked. Information systems are important to the organisation because they could help to reallocate scarce financial resources to other areas of the budget that needs them.

The State of IT within the organisation

The acting manager of the IT department noted that LSC is unable to appoint a permanent IT manager, since none of the applications received were suited to the job. They have been using IT for 15 years and are planning to improve the service to deliver an excellent service to their community.

The IT department resorts in the management services division and has 27 people working in the IT department. There are two sections in the IT department, i.e., the operational manager who controls computer operations and the networks and the systems development manager who controls system analysis and programming.

The IT manager noted that the City Council is happy with the present model of the IT department and that he believes that communication is fine between the IT department and the rest of the divisions at LSC. He stated that all IT staff knows what is defined as IT and that the City Council is happy with this definition.

They are using 486 machines as terminals in a Unix network. Their software consists of in-house developed and integrated software (e.g., Corel Perfect Office). All personal computer operators, end-users and managers have received appropriate training to use personal computers and the information they generate. LSC believes that IT should have maintenance contracts and made sure that their IT is covered by such contracts. The IT manager controls IT on behalf of the City Council.

Information Technology investment, benefit identification and post-implementation evaluation

LSC has a problem because they are working with a fixed IT budget of about R 1.5 million per annum. If the IT department needs to invest in IT they must motivate and re-motivate before the investment is finally approved. The City Council takes all decisions to buy assets (including IT) and approves all budgets. The Head of each division prepares motivations to buy these assets.

The IT department evaluate all motivations for IT investments and submits approved motivations to the financial division who will collate and submit the budget for final approval to the City Treasurer and eventually the City Council.

The fact that all IT investments have been motivated twice reduces the possibility of making mistakes during the budgeting period and ensures that all IT investments have been documented in detail. The IT or any other department submits IT investments. All these IT investments are discussed in detail with potential users before the actual IT investment are budgeted. These motivations could be in any format as long as they are well motivated. All IT investments have been coordinated with the interfacing functions. They measure the effect of IT by noting the effect of IT on LSC's turnover measured as an increase on turnover expressed as a percentage. They do not include hidden costs like cost of investigation nor do they include risk.

Financial criteria are an important to consider, because while evaluating any IT investments, LSC should ensure that they stay within the limits set by the Financial Division. The only management criteria they are applying is that the IT must deliver information fast and accurate. Development/technical criteria are applied by specifying that the IT investments must fit in with present hardware and software.

They would like to evaluate their IT investments better, but do not have the knowledge or manpower to do so. They do not have a breakdown of their IT costs in detail, since most of these costs are absorbed as part of other budgets, nor do they break IT costs down in the classification of IT supplied. The only post-implementation evaluation they perform is to measure how many customer and user complaints they receive. Threshold investments are handled as any normal investments.

They do not know what their key attributes should be and would like to undertake research in trying to find out how similar organisations handle these attributes. LSC also does not know how to use the technology aggressively without losing track of what they are about to achieve, i.e., to administer an efficient and effective service, thereby influencing the people to pay their rates.

SUMMARY

LSC noted that they would like to measure the productivity of the people using personal computers but does not know how to handle this. The case study highlighted that LSC was not really addressing the need to identify and measure benefits of IT investments and also to teach the people and departments to take responsibility for the IT investments allocated to them.

At this stage, there was no money available to do what they want to do. IT requires large sums of money and a task force of professionals, also a strong desire on the part of the City Council of LSC to get it working successfully. It is not clear to LSC how to achieve their ultimate goal or to link the organisational cultural climate of LSC to their IT strategy. These issues will have to be addressed by the City Council, but it might require a change in their IT strategy. LSC is still not in the clear on how to address these issues named.

Case Study 3: Financial industry:

The Buy Aid Society (BAS)

Introduction

The Buy-Aid Society (BAS) was founded by a consortium of consumers in Bloemfontein as a credit card operation. Presently BAS has agreements with more than 900 contractors, enabling their members to purchase a diverse number of goods while BAS receives a collection fee for the services it provides. BAS is small but it is run efficiently. The motto of BAS (*Because your family is important to you*) reflects their attitude to their members. BAS has three departments, i.e., financial, public relations, and computing; it employs a total of 15 workers.

In order to become a member of BAS, prospective members have to buy a minimum of two shares and goes through a normal application routine. Each member receives a monthly statement from BAS that reflects all purchases for the month. BAS guarantees payment of purchases by their members because they pay the accounts on their members behalf while they receive a collection fee from the vendors.

The collection fee is used to cover the running expenses of BAS and, at the end of each financial year, the surplus of the collection fee is distributed amongst members in good standing in the form of a bonus (a credit on their account) calculated as a percentage of their total purchases for the financial year. BAS also finances purchases for its members and sells insurance and funeral coverage to the members of the cooperative.

Organisational Strategy

BAS has a high standing in the market place in Bloemfontein achieved through a organisational strategy whereby they united the buying power of all it's members in such a way that their members achieve a savings on their purchases. The traders receive their money on time without having to worry about bad debts.

BAS believes that it differentiates itself in the market place in four main ways. These are:

- quality;
- range of services;
- good techniques;
- good people.

Quality of work is of importance to their clients and traders since it would ensure that all parties receive an accurate statement. In the areas of techniques, BAS is concerned with remaining a leader in the field by applying latest technology in Bloemfontein on their card (they have added a magnetic strip to their card), although BAS will not usually attempt to be a leading-edge practitioner. They would like to ensure that BAS delivers a good range of services to all parties. Their IT manager worked as part of a team that developed the system for them and was employed by BAS as IT manager.

Background to computing

BAS first moved into computing and office systems during 1989. Before this, they used a computer bureau to do their computer work for them (outsourcing). They used personal computers (IBM-compatible) with normal integrated software for the daily work installed on the personal computers hard drives. BAS started their own IT department in 1990 by investing into a Unix-box - a mini 200 level 60 computer supplied by ICL.

BAS asked for tenders that were to be submitted based on the requirements they had set and decided to accept the ICL tender because their tender was suited to meet the requirements set. They then started with systems development involving all parties, i.e., BAS staff, vendors and members. The completed system was thoroughly tested by BAS by running it parallel with the computer bureau. They tried not to duplicate systems and efforts across the organisation because they felt it might lead to redundancy. BAS only switched to the new system when they were sure that everything was running smoothly. By testing the new system in this way, they were sure that they would not waste the valuable time of BAS and their vendors and members. At this stage, they made an offer to their present IT manager, then to a member of the developing team, to become their IT manager. He accepted the offer and is running the IT department with three additional staff members.

The IT manager does all minor maintenance himself while ICL does all major work for them. All access to the system is on-line, although some of the vendors still use a manual system and their records and invoices are entered by BAS on their behalf. BAS is using an INTAC-bookkeeping system and the budget expenses of IT is R 32,500 per month.

The applications they are running are:

- word processing;
- list processing;
- accounting; and
- status processing.

The system was justified because BAS perceived that it will deliver strategic benefits, although specific and material these benefits are hard to quantify.

The main thrust of these benefits is that BAS will be able to sustain the high level of quality service they built their business on despite all new developments in the credit card business. They also expect the following tangible or quantifiable benefits:

- There will be a better market acceptance from proposals submitted. This will be due to the faster preparation of data, with more details that will be available from their database.

- The size of the IT department will be contained. They would not have to expand the IT department.

- Computer time will be generally well spent and this will lead to additional income.

While the new system was running parallel with the old system, they trained their staff and vendors to use it. This seemed to work fine. They selected their implementation team from suggestions by ICL. This team had regular meetings and gave feedback until everybody were happy. The equipment was installed with no real problems and all wiring was laid in the building and to vendors' sites with relative ease. All the initial planning paid off, although they did not attempt any post-implementation audit to date.

IT as an organisational resource

In addition to the number of people working at BAS, the expenses and assets, there is a fourth resource available to a functional organisation. This resouce relates to the support that a particular function can expect to receive from IT— investments in order to help BAS achieve its objectives. In this context, IT is being used to directly support the overall corporation strategies.

IT in the organisation

Communication is excellent between the IT department and the rest of the organisation because it is a small company. A clear IT definition exists and BAS is following the policy of centralised IT. The effect of IT could be viewed daily according to the IT manager; in fact, he added that their productivity will increase as soon as they completed the updating of a magnetic strip to their card. This would ensure that they become more computerised and increase productivity. Uses for IT are identified and discussed at weekly meetings of managers and if the use is worthwhile it will be implemented immediately. He stated that they at present have a good response time and better customer care.

IT investment procedures and benefit and IT investment criteria identification

The internal managers meet and take decisions to buy assets; smaller purchases of assets are approved internally, but substantial amounts must be approved by the members of the society. Motivations for these will be prepared by the manager of the department wanting to invest in the proposed asset. This motivation can be in any format as long as it is well motivated. The evaluation of IT investments is done by the IT manager.

If the IT department identifies a benefit in any IT investment, they ensure that BAS receives. They normally identify benefits visually and measure them by calculating the increase on turnover and by the decreasing number of complaints they received. BAS does not use any other method of measuring these benefits. They noted that it is also a problem to place IT investments if you work with fixed budgets, since major or threshold investments can only be approved by the members of the society at a special meeting.

BAS did not take any hidden costs into account as part of their IT investments. The risk of not having IT and not be able to run their business are fairly high. Most of the IT investments were tied to other investment strategies. BAS ensures that all IT investments fit in with the present interfacing functions.

BAS monitors the increased cash flow because of an IT investment placed and noted that this is the only financial criteria they use. Management criteria are measured by noticing customer satisfaction and information flow in the organisation. Development and or technical criteria are applied by ensuring that all new IT investments must fit in with their present hardware and software. These criteria are weighed by means of a gut feeling. They do not perform any post implementation evaluation of their IT investments. The IT department has a lot of freedom to respond to expectations.

BAS determines the priorities of different projects centrally because of the size of their organisation, and at the same time discovered that their IT investment projects cost more than originally budgeted. They try not to duplicate systems and efforts across the organisation because it might lead to redundancy. The IT manager is concerned that resources to implement and manage their IT are allocated tightly, cutting across all divisions and the annual budget cycle. They are concerned about uncontrolled operating costs and how this will affect the IT Department's budget. The IT manager feels that culture affects the use of their IT, but evidence is hard to find.

SUMMARY

BAS is a credit card organisation. The changes in their IT has ensured that BAS is maturing from being a small credit card to one of a developed organisation which has its own objectives, strategy, etc. This new outlook of BAS will bring with it a whole host of opportunities for the IT Department which in anticipation of these new challenges, ensures that the work is effectively performed.

Serenity Bank

Introduction and general background of the organisation

The Serenity Bank was formed in 1838. The Serenity Bank is an independent asset management, private banking and merchant banking group. Serenity Bank was established as a trust company by a group of prominent businessmen and has consequently been in operation for more than 157 years. During the last two decades, Serenity Bank has expanded its activities from those of a pure trust company to include private and merchant banking, pension fund management as well as a range of services, catering to the growing investment needs of both corporate and private clients. Serenity Bank was listed on the Johannesburg Stock Exchange in 1987 and is controlled by the Serenity Corporation Limited, which is in turn controlled by the Serenity Finance Company Limited and senior management.

This share holding structure enhances Serenity Bank's financial strength while allowing it to operate independently, thereby ensuring that the interests of Serenity Bank's clients are always paramount. It also enables Serenity Bank to attract and retain staff of the highest calibre. Serenity Bank has three major operating companies. These are Asset Management Limited, Private Bank & Trust Company Limited, and National Limited.

Serenity Bank claims that, as in 1838, their fundamental business is the provision of sound financial advice and the professional administration and management of client's assets. Their services are tailored to meet the needs of each client and this professional approach is backed by the technical resources of a modern financial services group.

Services offered by Serenity Bank

Serenity Bank offers a fund management service through its specialist management of investments on behalf of pension and provident funds. Most of these funds are managed separately; regular reporting takes place to keep clients informed on how their funds are invested and of their current value. Serenity Bank's general equity unit trust caters to investors seeking maximum growth of their capital. Serenity Bank also offer a balanced equity fund that caters for individual investors seeking steady growth and a higher income yield, and institutional provident and pension fund wishing to invest in a managed fund. Serenity Bank's income unit trust fund caters for investors seeking a regular above-average level of income and stability of capital.

Private Bank is a wholly owned subsidiary of Serenity Bank. Within the Private Bank, they offer investment management, financial planning, wills, estates and trusts, treasury, property finance and participation bonds and investments. National Limited is a joint venture between Serenity Bank and National Markets, the global corporate and investment banking division of the National Group. National Limited offers a wide range of financial services in the corporate, parastatal, and interbank markets. The bank is linked to global markets through he National Group.

Corporate governances

The directors endorse the Code of Corporate Practices and Conduct as set out in the King Report. During the period 1994/5, a full review of compliance with the Code was undertaken. This review indicated that the group largely complies with the Code, and in those instances where there was an opportunity for improvement, appropriate action has been taken. The directors have, by supporting the Code, recognised the need to conduct the group with integrity and accordance with generally accepted corporate practices.

Operational plan for IT at Serenity Bank

1995 was an interesting year at Serenity Bank and for the IT department. At the beginning of 1995, IT was in control of the information and applications; however, there has been an accelerated move towards employees controlling their information and applications. Office workers now create, use and share reports, memos and databases, tasks formerly employed by IS.

The IT mission of Serenity Bank today is adding business value. IT power in terms of control of IT is over. The IT structure is moving to provide support through help desks and development centres. Resources are shifting to Business Units, and IT resources to technical expertise and infrastructure providers and project resources, away from application designers. The IT culture is changing from the attitude that systems should conform to a defined set of standards to the attitude that they should meet user requirements.

The IT mission of tomorrow will be to provide an IT infrastructure, focus on providing and maintaining shared IT function and resources. The IT power will be based on its ability to add value to the business, while the IT structure will move to empowered self-managed teams. Hierarchical structures will break down, and develop into loose networks, virtual teams and matrix structures. Managing reuse of hardware, software and networks will become the focal point. Users will own systems, and be responsible for building, maintaining and supporting them. IT resources will be infrastructure providers, supplying the necessary objects, knowledge engineers, and coaches to assist users. Partnerships will be important. IT culture will change to an orientation of reusability.

IT in Serenity Bank

They have been using IT since 1970. The IT department does the following:

- strategic planning (define policies, procedures, standards, strategies and architectures and control the IT plan);
- resources management (capacity planning and IT procurement);
- service planning (recovery planning, security planning and service level agreements);
- resource control (change control, inventory control and database administration); and
- service control and development and maintenance (help desk, distribution, programming, etc.).

They use 13 staff members to control the hardware and the software. Currently Serenity Bank has an IBM RS/6000, an IBM AS/400, three XHP 3000s and seven NetWare file servers running LANs. All the IT are centralised. They have a fixed definition for IT, while the IT department controls all IT. Their IT staff has a combined total of 82 years of experience at Serenity Bank. They are running a diverse number of software, some of these are portfolio administration management software, databases, company analysis software and electronic fund transfer software. Their personal computers are running MSOffice,Lotus SmartSuite, Salaries software and other integrated packages. There are maintenance contracts for the IT. As it is not the intention of the case studies to investigate the number of software and describe them, a few were mentioned above.

IT investment and benefit identification

Serenity Bank cannot perform without IT and that is why all IT investments have been carefully planned. All vendors are carefully screened in terms of issues such as service contracts, client profiles and references, trading history, staff, location and branches, resources, managers and focus of the vendor. The software would be evaluated in terms of system requirements (i.e., server, workstations, network, applications and contracts). Other questions could be asked i.e., Does the package require its own server? What type of printers are required? Can you extract directly into Notes? They also visit sites where the vendor and the software are carefully screened (selection processes, expectations, budgets, knowledge, plans, contracts and the future are investigated).

The IT costs are normally in the region of R 9,000,000 per annum and is calculated as between 4 and 8% of the total group expenditure. They measure all benefits for IT investments in terms of productivity. They plan and monitor every IT investment to ensure that Serenity Bank will receive the benefits they identified before the time. The users department conducts an evaluation of the proposed IT investment while the IT policy committee approves the IT investments. Serenity Bank uses the portfolio approach to IT investment and the IT investments have been coordinated with other interfacing functions. Hidden costs are included as part of the costs of the IT investment. They mentioned that if IT does not increase productivity, Serenity Bank could experience a risk to the organisation. All IT are measured in terms of productivity.

Financial criteria are fairly important, but not a deciding factor. The increase of productivity are the most important management criteria they are using. Technical criteria are important when they consider any IT investment, it forms part of the evaluation process. The criteria are weighed according to the type of IT investment under consideration. They perform post-implementation evaluations by measuring productivity regularly.

SUMMARY

Serenity Bank's vision is to start central IT department that will provide operational, development and infrastructure services (e.g., server operations, development of common applications, marketing, consulting, education, planning, relationship management, and business analysis functions). The important key is the physical placing of IT staff within a Business Unit (BU). Problems that arise are role and responsibility disputes, questions of allegiance, contention over service level agreements, and architectural content. Some of the strengths of Serenity Bank's IT was that it had a stable system.

Case Study 4: Mining:

Mining Information Technology Division

Introduction

During 1967, a big mining group, controlling some gold mines in South Africa, decided to start its own information systems department, calling it Mining Information Technology Division (MIND). It was seen by mine management as an important strategic step in ensuring the continued successful availability of information to all its members.

MITD stated that the productivity tools supplied by the gold network system are of strategic importance to the gold mines for several reasons. The gold network, controlled by MITD, affects directly the working methods of the gold mines in such a way so as to produce productivity enhancements, as well as direct improvements in the effectiveness with which the mines produce their gold. The productivity enhancements will be derived from several sources, including the test that the IT tools provided by the system will dramatically increase speed of communications between the members of the mining group, i.e., between member mines, management and the bullion market, especially to help with the preparation of important documents such as proposals and reports.

The intermine services group of a this mining house has four arms, that is Drillers, TD, Stores and MITD. MITD controls the gold network on behalf of their Head Office, some gold mines and other relevant organisations. MITD supplies IT to these mines and on a bureau basis, provide a similar service to other clients. MITD is controlled by a manager who handles both the Financial Division and IT. MITD is made up of three departments (systems development, facilities management and EDI) employing 200 workers.

Organisational strategy

MITD is a large organisation with a strong tradition dating back many years. It has a high standing in the market place which it has achieved through an organisational strategy of differentiation. According to one of the senior people working in the IT division, MITD believes that it differentiates itself in the market place in these four ways:

- quality;
- range of services;
- good techniques; and
- good people.

Quality of work is of importance to the mines and MITD ensures quality through a system of management control. Another aspect of concern with quality is the importance placed on using only IBM personal computers. In the area of techniques, MITD is concerned with remaining in the lead in applying technology, although it will not usually attempt to be a leading-edge organisation.

Information Technology in MITD

MITD uses an IBM mainframe that can process at ± 78 MIPS, utilising about 190 Gigabyte diskpace. They calculated that they use their PCs at 95% capacity. MIND has classified IT and top managers and members agree with this classification. The costs of their IT (including staff) are ±R 14,000,000 per annum.

MITD only uses IBM and is happy with their IT. MITD is sure that the communication between them and the other departments and other divisions are satisfactory. There is a link between the IT strategy and the business strategy of the mines. MITD noted that they handle IT different from the way other organisations handle IT because they do capacity planning on a daily basis and can make instant decisions to expand. Service level agreements with their clients state that they will be up and running 98% of the time with a two-second wait state. This agreement could serve as the reason to upgrade machines to any platform that suit their agreements the best. MITDs computers are centralised with a file server and terminals at their clients' bases and their maintenance are decentralised. MITD recovers its costs totally by comparing the history of usage by its clients, monitoring its clients' uses and paying overcharges back to clients or recovering shortfalls. Facilities management determines which applications are used by their clients and calculate the unit cost by including all costs (e.g. line hire, etc.) but does not include hidden costs.

MITDs EDI department is probably their biggest operation—they are in touch with about 2,000 vendors using a direct order system while future planning includes the computerisation of tenders. MITD developed their own software in-house and sell software to other organisations. At this stage, about 400 organisations are using the software they developed.

The Facilities Department handles hardware and software support. Each of the previous named departments has one person in charge while a third person controls the operation and client services. The strategic plans of the organisation consists of supplying an IT service that will help the mines to maintain a profitable status. The main processes of MITD are to supply software and access to software with the necessary hardware platforms on which to run the software. The IT meet all the requirements set by their clients. MITD is sure that the communication between MITD and their clients are good.

Information Technology and MITD

MITD submits a fixed budget to the board of the mines and large extra-ordinary IT investments have to be submitted to a special meeting with a motivation that will convince the members that this service is vital to their needs. All motivations will be prepared by the section of MITD that wants to place the IT investment.

IT is purchased after they tested the relevant item and consulted all their members. The purchasing decision is taken and measured against benefits identified during the testing phase. These benefits could also be measured in a monetary form and increased productivity; they will, however, ignore intangible benefits. Therefore, they identify benefits before the implementation of the IT and can ensure that they receive these benefits.

These benefits are identified by comparing statements made by the vendor, checking specifications and using the IT themselves. MITD lists these benefits in their motivation to the board and by doing a post-implementation evaluation support the motivation originally placed before the board. They measure these benefits in terms of an over-collection from their clients and financial benefits. Costs of failure are reduced to a large extent, because they test IT before the time. They do not consider business risk to be part of their IT investment, since most of their costs are recovered. They do not tie IT investments to any other investment decisions.

Financial criteria are important because they use charge-back to recover all of the IT costs and would never overcharge their members. Management criteria are important because information must be supplied as accurately and up to date as possible to their clients. Development/technical criteria are applied in such a way by MITD that all software must fit in with the present hardware platforms and interfacing functions and that their clients do not wait longer than the wait state they claimed. No specific weights are allocated to any of the criteria as MITD follows a gut feeling most of the time. They are happy with their present evaluation process while threshold investments are handled as any other investment.

SUMMARY

The gold mining industry relies heavily on IT in virtually every aspect of its business, thus MITD uses IT in its efforts, its operational department, etc. As a result of this, MITD noted that IT can become an inhibitor to change, but they would like to know how to capitalise quickly on unexpected new opportunities. MITD also would like to improve economies of scale, i.e. to increase turnover with the same number of resources. However, as their clients do not have unlimited cash, MITD noted that there should be an annual review of migration opportunities and resources available.

Case study 5: Transport:

The period of 1940 to the 1970s were controlled by the then South African Railways and Harbours organisation, a government controlled organisation. They had a monopoly over all heavy-duty transport in SA.

Fast Transport

1.1.1.1 Background to the organisation

The transport industry is very competitive, and to be part of this industry, all information and control should be tight.. This organisation, Fast Transport (FT) also includes an abattoir (very diverse from the transport industry) and was founded in 1983.

FT is not a leader and they have a lot to learn. They employ 159 people and has offices throughout South Africa. FT is essentially split into two line functions —i.e., the abattoir and the transport operations. This case study focuses only on the heavy transport division. FT needs to do successful trading and to develop a professional approach to the marketing of both functions. It will not be easy to handle both, because both are in a very competitive field.

Strategy and Information Systems in FT

IT are used in FT, but not as extensively as they would like it to be. Mr. Minnaar explained that they have started to use IT intensively the last couple of years. It is beyond the scope of this case study to attempt to describe all, or even a large number of IT applications used by FT. This case study limits itself to looking at some aspects of how IT investment strategy is formulated. Before addressing the detail of this subject, it is important to consider the detail of some drivers which FT focuses and which are responsible for the organisation's strategy.

FTs current strategy is defined by their attempts to cope with the main drivers who propel the transport industry. These drivers have been particularly strong during the last couple of years since the government has allowed people other than TRANSNET to enter the transport industry and it is the same with the meat industry. Obviously, there are still rules and regulations that will control these industries. This transformation, which took place in a comparatively few years, can be attributed to the business drivers of the transport industry. Although there are several important drivers affecting the transport industry, by far the most important for FT is the arrival and steady development of competition. FTs drive is to capture a fair deal of the market. They are, however, not a significant player in the market and would like to increase this market share. Their decisions, thus, will not affect the competition as much, but they need to keep track of the decisions their competitors make.

Plans and budgets

There are several ways to achieve targets and goals that are expressed in their plans. They also need to do extensive business modelling that will enable them to evaluate alternatives. FT needs to inform their staff members of their individual and organisational targets and goals. These plans and budgets need to be expressed in terms of head count, expenses and assets required.

Resources available to make decisions

Historically, the important element in the firm's plan is the head count - the number of people who can be employed to complete the tasks. At the practical working level, this is the most rigidly controlled element in FT's plans and working procedures. All Heads of Departments are given a head count allowance within which they have to perform a task.

There is a reason why head count is considered to be of importance. This is because head count drives 60% to 70% of expense, and thus by controlling head count, expense can be controlled automatically. Each division will have to be told what it has to do over the next couple of years to achieve the target, and what resources are available. Each division should then produce its own plan and bring it back to the planning committee to enable FT to validate whether it can be achieved.

IT as an organisational resource

In addition to head count, expenses and assets, there is another resource available to divisions which relates to the support that a particular function can expect to receive from IT investment in order to help the division to achieve its objectives. In this context, IT is being used to directly support the overall organisational strategy. IT needs to view itself as a partner of the organisation to support it and achieve the stated objectives of FT and also that IT is a function expense-wise. FT should therefore ensure that IT is one of the efficient departments.

IT in the organisation

They have been using IT for 14 years. The IT forms part of the financial section while their auditors act as their IT consultants. These consultants ensure that ITs parameters are fulfilled. The communication is fine between all the departments in the organisation. IT is decentralised and the consultants control IT on behalf of the managing director. The architecture consists of a 486DX4-100 running a Novell 4 network. They use IT for accounting purposes, quotes and to keep track of their vehicles and other products they are selling. There are maintenance contracts for all the PCs. IT greatly affects the organisation because of its function in the organisation. The expense of IT is about R 100,000 per annum.

IT investment and FT

They measure the increase on turnover if they want to view the influence of IT. This measurement is calculated as a percentage. They are not including hidden costs and, while they take note of risks being part of any IT investment, would rather not include it as part of IT investments. IT has not been tied to any other investment strategies. The consultants submit IT investment projects and they are approved by the managing director. This presentation could be in any format and could also be submitted by other staff members. Financial criteria are considered because it was felt that IT could overspend their budget. The managing director would like to keep track of his heavy-duty tracks. They will consider special IT investments if it forms part of the normal architecture of FT. There are no special weight allocation to any of these criteria. They do not perform any post-implementation evaluation of any of the IT investments.

SUMMARY

They would like to increase the efficiency of their organisation, but do not know how to approach this with the help of IT. FT needs to invest more aggressively into IT, but they are not sure how this would affect their IT strategy. They would like to know how to do the best IT evaluation and benefit calculation to help them improve their business processes.

Although this case study has attempted to provide a brief insight into some of the issues that a large and sophisticated enterprise must manage in pursuit of the implementation of an IT investment strategy, the case study confirmed that IT has not addressed all the drivers responsible for making a firm look to its IT for competitive advantage. FT should consider how the organisation's structure could change due to the implementation of more and new sophisticated IT applications. FT needs to address these issues, and could thereby reduce costs and maintain a high level of consistency.

IPX

Background to the Organisation

IPX is part of the organisation that was solely responsible for transport before the 1990's. IPX was founded in Johannesburg in 1974. Their main business process is to provide information and IT to their mother organisation and the other branches of IPX. They are also responsible for business solutions in the organisation.

The transport industry has become very competitive and they need accurate and timely information, giving their organisation a competitive edge. IPX has four departments and 800 people working for them. These departments are: production, public relations, marketing and administration. They are a matrix organisation according to their organisational chart.

The transport industry had the notion that the Railway Corporation was too big and that other companies should share in the opportunities that exists in the industry. This action to spread the industry over a number of competitions tied up IPXs management with extensive planning and they are still planning on how to face competition.

Computing in IPX

They have been using computers since the inception of the organisation (1974), a total of 22 years. IPX is happy with the way IT is presently assembled, but IPX is preparing for the future and would like to keep an eye on the market to ensure that they increase their market share. IPX thinks that their communication is good and is also in the process of setting up bulletin boards to enable their clients and employees to communicate better. IPX linked their IS/IT strategy and the organisational strategy. IT enabled them to make decisions quicker and ensured that they can compute more solutions, helping IPXs managers to consider all possibilities and select the best solution to their business.

They think that there will be chaos if their organisation had no access to IT. Their definition of IT is accepted by top management. IPX stated that IT has fulfilled all promises made. The executive board of IPX controls IT fully. Their architecture consists of a combination of Persetel, IBM and AMDAHL main frames processing at 320 MIPS. They use software developed in-house and integrated software packages on their PCs. All computer operators and end users have been trained to use the IT to the best of their abilities and all managers have been trained to interpret the information they receive. The maintenance of computers have been attended to. The IT costs are in the region or R 5 million per annum with a yearly escalation of about 12%, depending on their plans for the year.

The IT investment approach and benefit identification process at IPX

They noted that IT greatly influences the performance of their organisation; they monitor the impact of computers on a regular basis in their organisation. IPX emphasised that this monitoring is done in a visual way and depends on a gut feeling of the manager. IPX sets targets for a specific month and measures how near they are to the target. The interviewer noticed that most of the time they reached a 95% target. IPX identifies a benefit only at the end of the month when they calculate the percentage change in turnover.

They ensure that they receive all benefits (financially) from service level and operational level agreements. They could not explain how this would accrue to them as they are not too sure - the impression was that they are looking at gut-feeling benefits. The benefits they identify might accrue from their projects plans. One of IPXs plans were scaled and it was noted that "...

[IT] provides the facilities necessary to develop all types of systems that one can wish to develop," but they do not substantiate statements made like the one. IPX includes hidden costs they identify as part of their IT investment. This is done by using their financial, human resources, and resources management program. There is no risk to IPX when they invest resources in IT. The only mistakes made when they propose an IT investment was that they seem to speak too much of technical jargon when they discuss IT. All their IT investments are tied to other investments as well as to their business objectives.

All IT investments have been planned and distributed to all the relevant people. IT investments could be submitted by their clients, project managers and project offices. They discuss all IT investments with potential users as well as with the managers concerned. IPX only accepts IT investment proposals prepared in the prescribed format. The evaluation of these projects are done by the client, project manager and project offices. They are not using the portfolio approach for their IT investments. Their investments have been co-ordinated with other interfacing functions. IPX does not know if they should use a top-down or bottom-up approach for IT investments. Also, if they want to be the best, they need to market themselves aggressively. Should they start using IT determinedly, they need to know how will this affect their IT investment policy and how they should approach these investments. With affirmative action being part of their organisational policy, they need to address the issue of organisational culture when they place IT investments. IPX would like to address their customer's wish for the benefits they would like to receive from IT investment.

Criteria and post-implementation evaluation

Financial criteria are used when they measure to see if the IT investment is still within their budget. They use project activities to measure management criteria when they evaluate the IT investment. Development/technical criteria are applied to ensure that the IT investment still uses the hardware and operating systems platforms created or are using. Weights are allocated to these criteria according to the importance of the project using a gut feeling. IPX tries to create an IT environment that would enable their clients to use a friendly system that is reliable. This is probably the most important reason for placing an IT investment. They are fairly happy with their present evaluation process.

IPX uses the same gut feeling to perform post-implementation evaluation and then supplements this with interviews, such as asking end-users if they are happy, then try to address any queries; at the same time, review the situation to find out if they have made the right decision to invest in IT. IPX noted that they have enough freedom to respond to expectations while doing any IT investment. IPX handles any threshold investments like normal investments.

SUMMARY

The case study has attempted to provide a brief insight into some of the issues that a large and sophisticated enterprise has to manage in the pursuit of IT investments and the benefit identification process. The case study has addressed the importance of the use of IT for competitive advantage and has noted how the organisation needs to address its requirements for change due to the implementation of sophisticated IT applications because they want to maintain their market share.

InterSA

General background to the organisation

The organisation was founded in 1976 and has three departments, i.e., administration, technical and business. InterSA is a carrier of passengers operating in the Free State. It owns a fleet of buses with which it competes with the taxi industry and all the other big names of passenger transport in SA. InterSA views its organisational mission as to be the best and the most successful company in the passenger transport industry and this will be reflected by a policy of safety and security, financial strength, service and value, and should be customer driven. To achieve these goals, InterSA believes that it must deliver a friendly and professional service. They should also search continually for improvements through innovation and the use of technology and strive constantly to achieve quality.

InterSA's strategy is one of differentiation, and it uses IT wherever possible to realise this strategy; therefore it achieves these objectives.

IT and InterSA

They would not like to improve on their present IT architecture of a 486 file server running a Novell network. The software is mostly outsourced for development and these are done according to the normal submissions of organisations from outside. They have been using IT for ten years and have a fixed definition of IT. InterSA noted that their IT and organisational strategy were not linked at present.

Their IT budget is in the region of R 200,000 per annum. The IT manager identifies needs and prepares all motivations for IT. InterSA measures the impact of computers by stating that they need accurate and timely information, which should help them to increase their productivity. Their directors stated that all information should be 100% accurate and although the information is historic of nature should help them to forecast the future trends of the industry with reasonable care. They measure mistakes in monetary values and noted that productivity would only be measured if they have to appoint more people to finish the same amount of work. InterSA uses salary savings as a form to convert the benefits of IT received into a measurement scheme.

The IT manager motivates and prepare evaluations of IT. She will specifically note any improvements on their present system and how it would be of benefit to the organisation. She felt that it was important that the organisation's directors be informed of the strengths of the IT department. There is a standard format for all these submissions.

InterSA considers technical criteria first of all before they consider management or financial criteria. They perform post-implementation evaluation because the IT manager needs to give feedback to the directors about the investment done and how it improved the productivity of the department. This must be done on a regular basis. Any deviation from the standard would have to be explained and improvements recommended.

SUMMARY

To ensure the loyalty of their workers, InterSA has developed a system whereby they try to computerise most of their operations, making it easier to do their jobs. This system is directed to enable the top management of the organisation to have reliable data and ensure that their staff is productive and accurate in what they do. This, however, requires resources which can assist them and give the directors confidence in what the workers do.

They need to do a regular technical check as the IT manager reported that they experience power failures. Their is also a phobia that the technology might be moving too fast for them and that they might lose the competitive advantage they have over their competitors. InterSA notes that their IT budget is not a problem as they control the IT costs tightly.

Case study 6: Property Industry:

House and Travel

General background to the Firm

The House and Travel organisation was founded in 1952. It has four directors and is based in Welkom (Free State). The IT department is located inside this building and forms part of the Financial Department. House and Travel's activities incorporate property development, rental, selling real estate and a travel bureau. House and Travel claims to handle 80% of all rentals in Welkom and they are selling a lot of real estate. All the divisions are running as one company, with each director managing at least one of the organisation's activities.

House and Travel is made up of ten departments and employs 50 people. They opened trust accounts for all the different processes and deposit money into these accounts for all property deals, rentals and travel bureau services. Their strategic plan includes the delivery of a good service to their clients by providing fast and accurate information.

The state of IT within the organisation

The four directors take and make decisions to buy assets. The relevant department prepares motivations for all asset acquisitions, while the accountant prepares motivations for acquisition of IT equipment. They have been using IT equipment intensely for six years. Their company is satisfied with the way their IT looks presently and no plans are under way to change the look of it. House and Travel is sure that the communication between IT and the rest of their departments are satisfactory. They also stated that their IT strategy and their business strategy is linked. IT, according to them, makes a major contribution to the organisation, in fact, they stated that the accounting department will grind to a halt if they did not have IT.

IT has fulfilled promises made and parameters have been set for IT classification. The four directors agree with this definition of IT, because they were involved in defining it. All their computers are centralised because they find it easier to control. The accountant controls all IT; he also installs their software. They are using a 486 DX 4-100 file server with 15 workstations (a Novell-25 user package). All end-users and managers have been trained to use the computers and the information generated by the computers. They also have arranged the maintenance of the computers. House and Travel estimated their IT expenses as R 500,000 per annum.

IT investment evaluation and benefits identification

According to them, IT affects the productivity and the accuracy of data. They could not tell how they measure productivity, they guessed that it might be because they do more work with the same number of people than a couple of years ago. House and Travel notes that its information is supplied accurately and on time to the managers and directors, one way to determine if IT has an affect on its business.

They also identify other benefits to the organisation by measuring the number of complaints they receive from their clients; apparently the number of complaints are down a lot and their customers seems to be a lot more satisfied. To ensure that they receive all the benefits from an IT investment, they write down benefits as part of the IT under consideration and at the same time, regard the IT in a holistic way. They do not include any hidden costs as part of their IT investments as they were not aware of these costs. They do not know of any risks to the organisation because they are using IT. They do not know how their medium and long term planning will fit in with the IT strategy. House and Travel is not aware of any mistakes made in the past while investing resources in IT and claimed that their IT investment decisions had been tied to other investment strategies, but could not explain how this was done.

House and Travel's accountant claims that all their IT investment decisions had been carefully planned and documented, but was not prepared to hand out a copy of this. The accountant would discuss IT investments with all the users and arrange a session with the vendors who would explain the advantages of the possible new IT investment. There is no standard format for all these proposals, as long as it is well-motivated. The accountant and the four directors evaluate these proposals while the final decision to invest is taken by the directors. They have never used the portfolio approach when they placed any IT investment. They made sure that their IT investments are coordinated with other interfacing functions, since they would like to ensure that their end users are confident when they use the computers.

Financial criteria are important when they consider any IT investment because they have to assure that it fit in with their budget. House and Travel's directors want to receive accurate and timely information and they place an emphasis on the data's integrity (management criteria). They use technical/development criteria because their hardware must support the software that they are using. There are no specific weights attached to any of the criteria they mentioned. The important reason for placing an IT investment is to ensure that House and Travel can still do their normal business. They are happy with the present evaluation process for their IT investments.

They claim that they perform post-implementation evaluation on how software or hardware is performing while they increase their yearly budget by 20% for upgrades. The accountant feels that he has enough freedom to respond to expectations. Threshold investments are handled in the normal way and they will finance their IT by using their reserve funds. House and Travel has a problem to measure the use of benefits from technology if they use it aggressively. They would also like to know if there is a guiding principle to ensure that they receive all benefits.

SUMMARY

They have a problem to coordinate the setting of IT investment goals with the goals set by their directors. House and Travel still does not know how they match their organisational culture to their IT investment culture and how their organisational culture affects the benefits they receive. The emphasis on the Internet was because they will reach overseas property investors. The indications are that they want to diversify their business but they need the knowledge on how IT will affect the business.

Case Study 7: Publishing:

Modern Newspapers

Introduction

Modern Newspapers is a medium-sized firm in the Northern Free State in South Africa. They publishes a wide range of weekly and monthly publications and other types of printing for people that needs this type of work to be done. There is competition from two other weeklies in the Northern Free State, but Modern Newspapers would like to increase their market share which it will believe will naturally result on an increased profitability, return on investment and cash flow. Although Modern Newspapers does not clearly articulate an organisational strategy, it is clear from observation that it pursues a niche strategy of being a cost leader.

IT in the organisation

They have been using IT since the inception of Modern Newspapers but they do not have a specific IT department as IT resides as part of the different departments that uses it. They have a well-defined definition for IT and the communication is fine between the different departments. All IT is decentralised and their architecture consists of 486 machines connected to a 486 file server running a Novell network. They uses mainly publication software.

As was to be expected, IT had been applied extensively to the production area in the newspaper organisation. Applications ranged from receipt of news to typesetting, page composition and layout. These applications had been well-received by the staff, who after appropriate training had achieved clear improvements in productivity. However, the organisation did not see applications as providing a competitive advantage, so much as ensuring that the company did not fall behind the technology, and therefore, the economic structure of the industry.

IT and benefits identification

The person that acts as their IT consultant decides on the architecture that they use. He has a degree, majoring in the Greek language and does not stay in the same town. He suggested to them that the main competitive edge application was their marketing system. The system was used by a team of salespersons who sold advertising space to some regular clients, as well as to many occasional advertisers in the weekly. Their database allowed them to administer the sales function more efficiently and effectively than previously and is believed to be one of the keys to Modern Newspapers' success. The system was not formulated as a strategic system but rather developed over a period of time as there was no specific implementation plan but rather a series of step by step upgrades. Each of these improvements required their staff to attend some training sessions.

The IT consultant prepares all motivations for IT, while the editor approves them after consultation with the parties that are going to use the proposed IT investment. They accept the consultant's proposal normally and are completely reliant on his expertise. He does not stay in the same town as the company. They do not include any hidden costs in this proposal. The proposals can be in any format, as long as it is well-motivated. There are a lot of risks involved because they are dependent on the consultant's suggestion. No criteria are considered as IT investments are done according to a gut feeling of all the parties. They could not define why they did specific investments, nor were they prepared to discuss the merits of any IT investment. They do not do any post-implementation evaluations.

The Nation's Paper

Introduction

The Nation's Paper is a medium-sized organisation publishing a wide range of daily, weekly and monthly publications. They also do other types of printing. The overwhelming objective of The Nation's Paper is to increase its market share, which it believes will naturally result in an increased objective, return on investment and cash flow. Although The Nation's Paper does not clearly articulate an organisational strategy, it is clear from observation that it pursues a strategy of being a cost leader in its area. The Nation's Paper has been in business for 101 years and has five departments (i.e., advertising, administration, circulation, technical and editorial).

As was to be expected, IT had been applied extensively to the production area in the newspaper area. Applications ranged from receipt of news to typesetting, page composition and layout. These applications had been well received by the staff who after appropriate training had achieved clear improvements in productivity. However, The Nation's Paper did not see such applications as providing a competitive advantage so much as ensuring that the newspaper fell behind the technology, and therefore the economic structure of the industry and their competitive advantage they have over their competitors.

IT in The Nation's Paper

They have been using IT intensively since 1984 when they bought their first IBM XT. Each section has their own network and because of this communication had not been good between the different departments. The IT and organisational strategy are linked; IT is decentralised. The editor controls all IT.

According to their IT manager, the strategic information system or competitive application was their sales and distribution database system. This system which operates on a 286-file server was used by the sales and circulation department who sold advertising space to some regular clients, as well as to many other advertisers in the newspapers. This database allowed them to administer the sales function efficiently and effectively and is believed to be one the key successes of The Nation's Paper. This system was not formulated as a strategic system, but grew out of a standard administrative software platform. Since this was developed over a period of time, there was no specific implementation plan, but rather a series of marginal step-by-step upgrades. Each of these improvements to the basic system had been accompanied by carefully planned and well-motivated training sessions.

IT investments

Their IT costs are in the region of R 1.5 million per annum. IT improves their productivity and they measure all benefits in terms of productivity. All IT investment proposals are approved by the board of directors. There is no standard format for any of these proposals, as long as they are well presented. The IT manager prepares the motivation and notes how it would help productivity, but does not include any of the hidden costs they identified. All IT investments are based on a needs assessment, while financial, management and technical criteria are taken into consideration. All benefits are measured in terms of productivity expressed in financial terms.

They perform any post-implementation evaluation of their proposed IT investments on a visual basis. For example, could people use the IT because, the IT manager noted, that some investments were just discarded after a while because of impracticality. They are investigating the possible pre-investment evaluation of IT to cancel all these losses because of the wrong IT investments placed.

SUMMARY

The Nation's Paper had implemented their IT over some phases. The case study highlighted that they experienced some losses because IT investments were not evaluated and that people invested in IT because they thought that IT would be the solution. They need improvements to their basic system, but these have to be implemented by changing their strategic planning for IT.

Case Study 8: Retailing Industry:

Knockers

Introduction

Knockers is a retailing organisation founded in Bloemfontein in 1968. They have 42 different departments. During 1985, a committee of the directors gave the final go-ahead to purchase a Sperry mini-computer. The system was endorsed by the managing director. They are presently contemplating the upgrading of their system in the nearby future.

Knockers considers that the help they received from this system are of particular strategic importance to the firm for several reasons. The system affected the working methods of the organisation directly in such a way so as to produce substantial productivity enhancements, as well as direct improvements in the effectiveness with which the firm can control their stock. They also increased speed of communications between members of the directors and their top management, especially in the preparation of key documents such as stock reports and monthly financial statements.

Organisational Strategy

Knockers is a large organisation with a long tradition of low prices dating back many years. It has a high standing in the market place in Bloemfontein achieved through an organisational strategy of differentiation. According to one of the directors, Knockers believes that it differentiates itself in the market place in the following ways. These are:

- quality;
- good prices;
- efficient salespersons;
- range of goods offered.

Quality of work is of importance to Knockers and the firm ensures quality through a two-tiered system of management control. Another aspect of control is the with quality is the importance placed on selecting the best goods for their organisation at the best price available. All the directors have a good working knowledge of IT, and there is a positive attitude towards its use in the firm.

Background to computing

Knockers first moved into office systems and stock control in 1985 with the purchase of a Sperry minicomputer running a Unix operating system serving four terminals and the cash registers in the shop. Prior to that, the firm had relied on outside firms to help them with their computing needs. It is not known when the first personal computers were used in the firm, but they were original IBM-compatible machines. These machines had been introduced into the firm on an on-demand basis and by 1985, had been used with a number of word processing packages as well as different spreadsheets and databases. There was a mixture of hardware and software and difficulties were frequently experienced with having the right data for the right software for the right machine. The connectivity of these systems had not been extensively pursued by the firm.

The minicomputer was installed because Knockers felt the need to computerise their organisation. The applications run on this mini computer is Impact and Pastel. They still use IBM-compatible machines for word processing. In addition, the Sperry mini is used for electronic banking and funds transfers.

IT investment

They regard the investment in the Sperry minicomputer as one of their better investments. Their IT costs are normally in the region of R 140,000 per annum. The directors make the decision if they want to extend or upgrade the present system. All proposals will serve before the board of seven directors and they will discuss the proposals in detail. They are, however, not in the position to determine the effect of computers on Knockers. They are aware of hidden costs, but do not include it as part of their IT investment expenses. All the IT investments were tied to other investment strategies. The proposals for any IT investment could be in any format but must be well motivated, stipulating the benefits it could incur and how the benefits would be measured. The IT director submits IT investment proposals and will place the IT investment after the board of directors has approved it.

Knockers notes that the Sperry-mini computer system ensures that their business runs effectively. They measure the benefits they receive from their IT investment in terms of productivity (a visual measurement). They note that work is finished sooner and the information available earlier, enabling Knockers to act sooner and get an edge on their competitors. They do not consider any risks as being part of their IT, but are aware of the risks.

Any IT investment should meet the development and technical criteria set before they would approve it. Any deviation from this criteria would have to be specially motivated. The importance of management criteria was mentioned because Knockers believes that the information they should get from the IT investment should be accurate and timely. There are no specific weights allocated to any of these criteria, although they might be considered in the order named above.

They do not do any detailed post-implementation evaluation, except to measure the increased productivity. The emphasis on productivity was placed because it enabled all the workers to finish their work on time or sooner. This helps Knockers to improve the competitive edge they have over their competitors.

Overview of the case

The directors of Knockers noted that support for the IT investment could increase as the system gets older. They, however, feel that they are still getting their money's worth from the investment. They also realise that they will have to replace it and are making contingency plans to do so within the next five years. The need was expressed during the investigation that people should be trained and an emphasis placed upon the use and information that could be gained from the IT investment. Knockers needs to put in a lot of work to keep their place in the market. They realise that technology will help them to keep the competitive edge and use their organisational strategy to plan their IT investment for the future. Their planning seems to be correct, but they will need their organisational culture and integrates it with their IT to ensure that they will survive.

Builders

Introduction to Builders

Builders is a large chain of hardware stores in the Free State, employing 270 people, selling various products which are used in and around the house. They are in a competitive market and there is ample opportunity for the firm to differentiate its products. Although they believe themselves to be very efficient, their record does not show it.

Builders is a firm with a clearly generic strategy which has worked for the business for many years. This strategy is that of cost leadership, and to this end it has used IT very successfully. Builders is highly computerised, both from a stock control point of view, as well as with more traditional data processing applications. However, the law of diminishing marginal returns set in with respect to their cost reduction efforts using IT; As a result, IT management started to look to other, non-cost reduction, IT opportunities from which the firm might benefit.

IT in the organisation

Builders has been using IT intensively for ten years. The interest in strategic information systems was initiated by the managing director who has a long and distinguished career with the firm. During his time with the organisation, he has built a highly successful IT department which is driven by a cost containment culture. This is reflected in a structured financial approach to system approval. This managing director became aware of what some competitors were doing with their IT; he believed that Builders must follow suit if it was not to fall behind. In addition, it was felt that if they used strategic information systems they might obtain some protection from the increasing phenomenon of other overseas competitors who periodically dump products in the market. Therefore, competition activities was the primary driver making Builders look for strategic information systems.

With the above mentioned in mind, they defined IT's parameters. Also, because of the competitive market they are in, it was decided that the IT department should communicate well with other departments. Their IT is decentralised with a central file server. Their architecture consists of a mainframe running Chameleon. They maintain the equipment with the help of maintenance contracts because they cannot afford to lose any business time.

IT investment approaches by Builders

All motivations for IT investments are prepared by the managing director or a person he designates. He approves all motivations and if he feels that he would have to consult the board of directors, he would do the presentation as well. The presentation could be in any well-presented format. Benefits might be identified before the time, but if the investment is crucial to the business then they would not bother with it.

Their IT costs are normally in the region of R 120,000 per annum. They also noted that their business activities would grind to a standstill if the computers are down. They measure benefits in financial terms, but do not calculate any ratios. The managing director mentioned that there was not a concurrence of views as to the objective of the strategic information systems among the directors. In addition, confusion set in with regards to the firm's objectives, which were its strategy and critical success factors. They also do not include hidden costs in their IT investments.

Development and technical criteria were the important criteria to be considered. If any of the proposals do not complement the present system, they will discard it. The financial and management criteria were judged to be of equal importance when any IT investment was being evaluated. They do not perform any post-implementation evaluation.

SUMMARY

The managing director noted that ideally, they would like to visit sites of similar investments under consideration by them. It is, however, sometimes crucial that the proposed IT investment be placed as soon as possible. The after sales service and product should also be considered. These issues would be brought into the process as soon as possible with their future IT investments.

The case study focuses on a number of issues which must be addressed when formulating an IT investment policy which would lead to its successful IT investment for Builders and the successful use of it. It primarily highlights a number of issues which should have been kept in mind when any IT investment are under consideration.

Case Study 9: Couriers:

The Fast Courier

Background

The Fast Courier was started 12 years ago. It has three and a half divisions, an express parcel division, fast freight division, retail division and a small half division (Fast Courier is calling it a half division) that they still want to develop. Last year they appointed an IT director who was given a free hand to improve the IT because the business was dependent on IT. The Fast Courier is one of many courier services in South Africa. The Fast Courier has been set IT targets and, should they not reach it, would lose some of their market share (if not all).

The Fast Courier is in the process of a major reorganisation, divisions are being re-organised as separate arms with chief executives, etc. The main objective of this reorganisation is to ensure that the business divisions would improve their performance by focusing directly on issues of their own profitability and accountability. The IT department has been centralised and they expect to increase the impact of computers over the next couple of years.

IT in the Fast Courier

They have been using IT for 12 years and very intensively the past two years. The IT director is in charge of IT, with three managers reporting directly to him. The three managers are responsible for business support systems, systems infrastructure and development. There are 30 people working in the IT department presently. The IT director forms part of the executive committee of the Fast Courier organisation. The Fast Courier is established in the courier business and it is believed that IT will play an important role in the strategic planning of the firm. Their current IT budget is R 6 million. The present organisational focus is the IT department and they have been asked to develop IT.

The IT director prepares all motivations and takes it to the executive committee of the organisation. Because the focus is on IT, their idea is to determine if IT has any influence on the organisation. The IT department has presented their two-year strategic plan and they are following the proposed procedure. All benefits to the organisation had been decided up front and the message was that, should IT not reach the set goal, the organisation would also be down the drain. Strategic information system opportunities had been identified by the Fast Courier and were formulated in detail in a formal way. This resulted because the IT director perceived an opportunity by extending the functionality of the current system and convincing management of the value of the project. When they implemented the proposed systems, they were treated the same as any other IT project; the issue of ease of use and the end-user training was strongly emphasised.

Plans and budgets

There were several ways to achieve the targets and goals set by the executive committee which were expressed in product plans and revenue plans. Extensive business modelling was performed to evaluate alternatives. Eventually, they agreed to a particular scenario and there were a cascade of these organisational targets into functional target areas. Each director was told what to do and that required plans and budgets to be exploded into the next level of detail for each functional head. These plans and budgets are expressed in terms of three resources: head count, expense and assets required.

IT investment issues

They do not include any hidden costs as part of the calculation of their IT investments. The story was relayed that they invested into a special weighing machine. This machine's costs were in the region of R 600,000. Parcels were being weighed again because customers did not tell the correct weight and the extra costs were recovered from the clients. This machine paid for itself within six months and they thought that they were on a good track until one of the drivers wrote the machine off in a moment of carelessness.

Because the future of the organisation is tied to all IT investments, the policy was that all these investments should be set out in detail explaining all benefits and advantages of the specific investment. That is why the board needs to approve all investments. There is no standard format for any of these proposals as long as it is well-presented. The total IT budget had been set as R 10 million over two years. Management criteria therefore weighs the most followed by the financial and technical criteria. They do not deem technical criteria to be to important at this stage, since all IT investments are part of the initial proposal. They, because they are in the process of the IT investment stage of two years, are not doing any post-implementation evaluations and it is envisaged to do a follow-up study to find out if the process worked for The Fast Courier.

SUMMARY

The IT director seems very keen on making sure the IT department works out fine. The Fast Courier has learned lessons all along. The also noted that all IT investment should be regarded as a complete picture. The overall IT picture for the business should help people decide if they want to invest in IT or not. The Fast Courier has to survive in a competitive field and any bad decisions should be avoided as they cannot afford to lose any business. They are viewing themselves as leaders in the field and would like to strengthen their position. This would require their IT department to be on the right track making the right investments and ensuring that they would still be there tomorrow. Their IT developments had been described as one of the most exciting developments of the courier business. All these dimensions of IT were addressed, i.e., functional partner, the IT strategy for optimising its own performance and the IT department as a functional partner.

Case Study 10: Construction:

Construction Company

The Construction Company is a large firm, employing 800 people, producing various buildings, roads and other constructions. They are in a competitive market and there is little opportunity for the firm to differentiate their products as most construction are done according to a fixed plan. They believe the organisation is efficient.

Construction Company is a construction firm with a clear strategy which has worked for them for 34 years. This strategy is of cost leadership, and to this end it has used IT very successfully. The firm is highly computerised both from a construction point of view, as well as with more traditional data processing applications. However, they have appointed a computer shop as their IT consultants and, as a result, because they relied heavily on this consultant and his advice, have experienced that their IT costs are running away. This consultant prepares all motivations when the IT manager (the managing director's wife) has notified them what they need the IT for. They accept the consultant's advice and buy the proposed IT without asking for a second quote. One of the employees noted that, no matter what the cost, they ensure that they will get it and, at the same time, stated that the Construction Company loses IT opportunities.

They do not have an IT strategy in place and, although their IT seems to be running smoothly, are lacking a financial approach to systems approval. The IT manager is adamant that they would lead the way and is trying her utmost to ensure that their system is the best, even if it is not what they need at present.

Their architecture consists of a 486-file server running a 25-user Novell network. The IT costs are R 180,000 per annum and they measure benefits by calculating the computer costs for the construction divided by the percentage profit of each construction as a ratio. The Construction Company does not include hidden costs as part of their IT investments. All IT investments are prepared in the form of a quote after the IT manager has faxed their needs through to the computer shop. If any IT investment does not do what they require it to do, they actually will ask the IT consultant to replace it and ensure that the IT investment actually delivers what it promised to do.

No strategic opportunities were identified by The Construction Company and none of these opportunities were documented. No IT strategy exists and one of the employees expressed doubt that the IT department is supporting the firm's goals. The need was expressed that the functionality of the IT department should be investigated and changes made.

No post-implementation evaluation, other than the inquiry about the functionality of the IT was ever done. The IT budget is approved and drawn up by their internal auditor. This budget is escalated every six months, ensuring that all processes are updated and projects scaled for new equipment. They do not consider any criteria according to the IT manager and the employees that were interviewed. They experience a problem with computer literacy, but this does not hamper their attitude that they must have the best.

Corrugated Corporation

Corrugated Corporation is one of the largest firms of construction and plant hire in the Free State. In common with most of the players in its industry, it operates with a strategy of differentiation, offering a fast response to its clients. There have been some factors that have lead Corrugated Corporation to move towards computerisation and specifically towards strategic information systems. The first is the turbulence experienced with the change of the government; the second is the awarding of contracts to mainly black organisations or organisations that practice affirmative action. This has resulted in construction companies looking for much more control as well as greater insights into the type of risks that they are taking. Also deregulation has meant much greater competition. Corrugated Corporation feels that its current systems, designed to serve the needs of their clients, require greater integration. These drivers have resulted in the revision of their IT investment policy. The accountant identifies and evaluates all IT investments, while at the same time considers the needs they identified above.

These proposals could be in any format as long as they are well-formulated. The Corrugated Corporation was founded in 1967 and started to use IT intensively in 1990. Their IT is well-defined and the IT strategy and the organisational strategy is linked. The IT is centralised. It is envisaged that they could decentralise IT and connect all sites by modem with the new IT policy they are in the process of setting.

The IT costs are about R 60,000 per annum. They do not include any hidden costs as part of any IT investment. They measure the benefits of IT in terms of productivity (work is finished sooner) but this is done on a visual basis. All IT investment proposals could be in any format, as long as they are well formulated.

Because they are in the process of developing their IT to suit the new strategy they devised, it is expected to last over a period of time; they have a specific implementation plan. They noted that the future implementation of IT is to be a series of marginal upgrades. All future IT investments are to be viewed as a global picture whereby they run their operational plan and the IT strategy in parallel. All these upgrades and improvements would have to be planned carefully and all aspects (including training) would have to be taken into consideration.

Case Study 11: Electronics:

Freddies Instruments

Freddies Instruments is one of the larger manufacturers and reconditioners of electronic measuring instruments in South Africa. The deputy-managing director (now managing director) employs many people in all their branches. In addition, Freddies Instruments traditionally has held itself aloof, being a market maker and standard setter rather than a market responder. However, the last couple of years has seen dramatic changes in the electronics industry with the fundamental economics of instrument manufacture and marketing radically shifting. This has resulted in more electronic manufacturers manufacturing instruments for a fraction of what it cost them a couple of years ago. These drivers have resulted in a major cultural change in Freddies Instruments which are directly reflected in the way Freddies Instruments uses its own internal IT resources. Thus, Freddies Instruments has identified how they can make extensive use of IT to support its business strategy. This is reflected in its manufacturing systems, its data processing systems, its tools systems, as well as various strategic networks, the support of product sales and maintenance of their larger systems.

Freddies Instruments has identified some strategic IT issues on which to focus. The first of these relates to how the IT department acts as a technology partner by helping other departments to implement IT, in order to gain a competitive advantage. One of the other aspects mentioned by the managing director is how it develops strategies or policies for its own survival within the organisation. Thus at this stage, Freddies Instruments does not have a detailed hardware and software strategy. They have installed a new mini-computer and one of the employees commented that the IT is now really working. The managing director himself proposes all IT investments and makes the decision to implement the decision. According to him, this *hardball* policy was needed and will have to be changed once everything is working well.

The few strategic information system opportunities were identified by Freddies Instruments' managing director, but were not formulated in any formal way. This resulted from opportunities identified by him and included because a stronger emphasis was given to the issue of ease of use and training the end-user.

They do not measure any benefits because the managing director deemed the decisions he made to be an emergency control. The major risk he had to face was that the IT investment might not work out and could be a disaster. There are no cost-benefit calculations or any other benefit identification exercise. The managing director commented that they need to set a formal IT investment procedure, but it would require a strategic meeting specifically set to plan this. They would accept any proposal as long as it is well-motivated. They do not perform any post-implementation evaluation. The managing director noted that IT should control the business, but they need to plan how this should be done. Freddies Instruments needs to set a formal IT strategy.

ENDNOTES

[1] Goldfields are a region in the Free State province of SA. It is a predominantly gold mining community.

[2] Unischool and Academy of Learning are programmes for people who cannot afford to go to a Technikon or University.

APPENDIX B

Presentation of the Statistical Calculations Used to Create the Correspondence Analysis Figures

Correspondence analysis

Data range : Workbook = CH5REAS.XLS / Sheet = Sheet1 / Range = d2..o9

Testing hypothesis of independance between rows and columns:

Chi2 distances on data = 90.6080 ~ degrees of freedom = 60

Limit Chi2 for the chosen confidence range = 79.0820

Using this test, one should reject the hypothesis of independence

Eigenvalues and corresponding inertia :

Eigenvalues	1	2	3	4	5	6
Values	0.1371	0.0788	0.0299	0.0198	0.0082	0.0000
inertia %	50%	29%	11%	7%	3%	0%
cumulative	%50%	9%	90%	97%	100%	100%

Row-profiles coordinates on factorial axes :

	1	2	3	4	5	6
OS	0.0064	0.3150	0.0832	0.0813	0.1139	-0.0020
MD	-0.0324	0.3146	-0.0260	-0.0782	-0.0791	0.0049
FB	0.7442	-0.2833	-0.0034	0.1262	-0.0201	0.0018
QS	-0.5497	-0.1563	-0.2604	0.1799	-0.0351	-0.0012
IF	-0.2402	-0.1460	0.3406	-0.0237	-0.1239	-0.0047
MS	0.3175	0.0742	-0.2544	-0.2491	-0.0178	-0.0080
EI	-0.3079	-0.4523	0.0477	-0.2297	0.1462	0.0042

Column-profiles coordinates on factorial axes :

	1	2	3	4	5	6
I1	-0.0191	0.7369	-0.0381	0.0219	0.0686	-0.0029
I2	0.2042	0.3436	-0.4695	-0.0213	-0.2163	0.0179
I3	0.1171	-0.1276	-0.1053	-0.2644	-0.0776	-0.0046
I4	-0.1944	-0.0591	0.2847	-0.1800	0.1079	0.0060

I5	0.4776	-0.2077	-0.0494	0.1287	0.0623	-0.0001
I6	-0.7534	-0.1670	-0.0726	0.1299	-0.0239	-0.0010
I7	0.3228	0.1783	0.5701	0.1879	-0.3018	-0.0013
I8	0.0115	0.5751	-0.4622	-0.4748	-0.2708	-0.3404
I9	-0.1842	0.7109	0.6427	0.0135	-0.1092	-0.0964
I10	-0.0352	1.1212	0.1654	0.0113	0.1926	0.3488
I11	0.0569	-0.0757	-0.1514	-0.0625	0.0718	-0.2735

Row Contributions
to factorial axes inertia

	1	**2**	**3**	**4**	**5**	**6**
OS	0.0001	0.2804	0.0516	0.0746	0.3540	0.0535
MD	0.0017	0.2737	0.0049	0.0674	0.1671	0.3075
FB	0.5362	0.1351	0.0001	0.1070	0.0065	0.0268
QS	0.2822	0.0396	0.2902	0.2096	0.0193	0.0102
IF	0.0479	0.0308	0.4412	0.0032	0.2136	0.1510
MS	0.0697	0.0066	0.2052	0.2977	0.0037	0.3586
EI	0.0623	0.2337	0.0069	0.2405	0.2358	0.0924

Column Contributions to factorial axes inertia

	1	2	3	4	5	6
I1	0.0003	0.7508	0.0053	0.0026	0.0629	0.0553
I2	0.0086	0.0426	0.2096	0.0007	0.1629	0.5413
I3	0.0133	0.0274	0.0492	0.4696	0.0979	0.1661
I4	0.0288	0.0046	0.2826	0.1710	0.1487	0.2250
I5	0.3313	0.1089	0.0163	0.1670	0.0947	0.0001
I6	0.5889	0.0503	0.0251	0.1213	0.0099	0.0086
I7	0.0288	0.0153	0.4120	0.0677	0.4229	0.0037
I8	0.0001	0.3381	0.5756	0.9192	0.7237	554.3201
I9	0.0141	0.3647	0.7855	0.0005	0.0830	31.3664
I10	0.0002	0.3023	0.0173	0.0001	0.0861	136.9355
I11	0.0021	0.0065	0.0690	0.0178	0.0569	400.1063

Squared cosines of angles between row vectors and under-spaces

	1	2	3	4	5	6
OS	0.0003	0.7888	0.0551	0.0526	0.1032	0.0000
MD	0.0093	0.8751	0.0060	0.0540	0.0554	0.0002
FB	0.8515	0.1234	0.0000	0.0245	0.0006	0.0000
QS	0.7060	0.0571	0.1584	0.0756	0.0029	0.0000
IF	0.2735	0.1011	0.5499	0.0027	0.0727	0.0001
MS	0.4317	0.0236	0.2773	0.2658	0.0014	0.0003
EI	0.2522	0.5444	0.0061	0.1404	0.0569	0.0000

Squared cosines of angles between column vectors and under-spaces

	1	2	3	4	5	6
I1	0.0007	0.9872	0.0026	0.0009	0.0086	0.0000
I2	0.0975	0.2760	0.5153	0.0011	0.1094	0.0007
I3	0.1172	0.1392	0.0948	0.5972	0.0515	0.0002
I4	0.2271	0.0210	0.4870	0.1947	0.0700	0.0002

I5	0.7755	0.1466	0.0083	0.0563	0.0132	0.0000
I6	0.9182	0.0451	0.0085	0.0273	0.0009	0.0000
I7	0.1774	0.0541	0.5533	0.0601	0.1551	0.0000
I8	0.0001	0.3448	0.2228	0.2350	0.0765	0.1208
I9	0.0348	0.5190	0.4242	0.0002	0.0122	0.0095
I10	0.0009	0.8702	0.0189	0.0001	0.0257	0.0842
I11	0.0280	0.0495	0.1979	0.0337	0.0446	0.6463

Correspondence analysis

Data range : Workbook = CH5BENE.XLS / Sheet = Sheet1 / Range = d2..o9

Testing hypothesis of independance between rows and columns:

Chi2 distances on data = 60.2232 ~ degrees of freedom = 60

Limit Chi2 for the chosen confidence range = 79.0820

Using this test, one cannot reject the hypothesis of independance

Eigenvalues and corresponding inertia :

Eigenvalues	1	2	3	4	5	6
Values	0.0974	0.0407	0.0226	0.0063	0.0008	0.0001
inertia %	58%	24%	13%	4%	0%	0%
cumulative %	58%	82%	96%	99%	100%	100%

Row-profiles coordinates on factorial axes :

	1	2	3	4	5	6
PB	0.2258	0.0832	0.1126	-0.0745	-0.0241	0.0081
NO	0.2106	-0.0156	-0.0860	-0.0555	0.0201	-0.0167
CB	-0.4425	0.3604	-0.1071	0.0218	0.0102	0.0047
CA	0.0087	-0.1959	0.1339	0.0267	0.0550	0.0136
CO	-0.5659	-0.2206	0.1653	-0.0239	-0.0217	-0.0113
IC	0.0065	-0.3168	-0.3031	0.0286	-0.0289	0.0112
RR	0.3929	0.0782	0.1479	0.2598	-0.0258	-0.0116

Column-profiles coordinates on factorial axes :

	1	2	3	4	5	6
I1	-0.4437	-0.4516	0.0316	0.0481	-0.0131	-0.0002
I2	-1.5495	0.8265	-0.1081	0.0827	-0.0150	-0.0566
I3	-0.2727	0.1955	-0.0340	-0.0906	-0.0264	0.0223
I4	0.4951	-0.0241	0.0355	-0.0507	-0.0644	-0.0161
I5	0.0676	-0.0190	0.0654	-0.0818	0.0384	-0.0054
I6	0.2205	0.0396	-0.2697	0.0930	0.0126	0.0025
I7	0.1668	0.2160	0.4057	0.1786	0.0032	0.0085
I8	0.0624	-0.3124	0.4510	-0.4856	0.1926	-0.1788
I9	-0.1380	-0.5632	0.2698	-0.3338	-0.0339	0.0023
I10	-0.5691	-0.5854	0.2637	-0.5015	-0.0278	-1.1913
I11	-0.0183	-0.0862	0.1949	-0.4296	-0.2191	0.1700

**Row Contributions
to factorial axes inertia**

	1	2	3	4	5	6
PB	0.1257	0.0408	0.1346	0.2129	0.1720	0.1148
NO	0.0960	0.0013	0.0688	0.1035	0.1053	0.4238
CB	0.2660	0.4225	0.0670	0.0100	0.0170	0.0209
CA	0.0001	0.1202	0.1010	0.0145	0.4770	0.1717
CO	0.4189	0.1524	0.1539	0.0116	0.0741	0.1186
IC	0.0000	0.2540	0.4179	0.0135	0.1062	0.0932
RR	0.0932	0.0088	0.0568	0.6339	0.0482	0.0570

**Column Contributions
to factorial axes inertia**

	1	2	3	4	5	6
I1	0.2278	0.5653	0.0050	0.0417	0.0239	0.0000
I2	0.3624	0.2469	0.0076	0.0161	0.0041	0.3415
I3	0.0861	0.1059	0.0058	0.1478	0.0971	0.4070

I4	0.2220	0.0013	0.0049	0.0363	0.4520	0.1665
I5	0.0101	0.0019	0.0408	0.2306	0.3931	0.0447
I6	0.0734	0.0057	0.4727	0.2032	0.0290	0.0066
I7	0.0182	0.0731	0.4633	0.3244	0.0008	0.0337
I8	0.0020	0.1176	0.4405	1.8453	2.2480	11.3433
I9	0.0153	0.6115	0.2522	1.3952	0.1116	0.0031
I10	0.0652	0.1652	0.0603	0.7873	0.0188	201.4030
I11	0.0003	0.0179	0.1645	2.8883	5.8211	20.5152

Squared cosines of angles between row vectors and under-spaces

	1	**2**	**3**	**4**	**5**	**6**
PB	0.6641	0.0901	0.1651	0.0723	0.0075	0.0009
NO	0.7958	0.0043	0.1325	0.0552	0.0072	0.0050
CB	0.5798	0.3845	0.0339	0.0014	0.0003	0.0001
CA	0.0013	0.6361	0.2975	0.0118	0.0502	0.0031
CO	0.8058	0.1225	0.0688	0.0014	0.0012	0.0003

IC	0.0002	0.5172	0.4734	0.0042	0.0043	0.0006
RR	0.6159	0.0244	0.0873	0.2693	0.0026	0.0005

Squared cosines of angles
between column vectors and under-spaces

	1	**2**	**3**	**4**	**5**	**6**
I1	0.4869	0.5045	0.0025	0.0057	0.0004	0.0000
I2	0.7730	0.2200	0.0038	0.0022	0.0001	0.0010
I3	0.6039	0.3103	0.0094	0.0667	0.0057	0.0040
I4	0.9653	0.0023	0.0050	0.0101	0.0163	0.0010
I5	0.2626	0.0208	0.2457	0.3847	0.0847	0.0016
I6	0.3690	0.0119	0.5521	0.0657	0.0012	0.0000
I7	0.1026	0.1722	0.6072	0.1177	0.0000	0.0003
I8	0.0064	0.1601	0.3335	0.3867	0.0608	0.0524
I9	0.0365	0.6081	0.1395	0.2136	0.0022	0.0000
I10	0.1345	0.1423	0.0289	0.1045	0.0003	0.5895
I11	0.0011	0.0242	0.1236	0.6007	0.1563	0.0941

Index

R

S

T

V

About the Author

Sam Lubbe has spent more than 12 years working in the field of information systems. He has served some time as a user and as an IT professional. He always ensured that the organisations obtain the maximum benefit for the amount of money they invested in IT.

Recently he has specialised in the area of IT investment evaluation and benefit realisation. He has published articles in this subject area. He holds a B.Com., B.Com. (Hons.), M.Com and Ph.D. and is a Senior Lecturer at Vista University in South Africa.

$49.95

AB 17/6/99

Information Technology Diffusion in the Asia Pacific: Perspectives on Policy, Electronic Commerce and Education

Idea Group Publishing